JL
DY

HOURS OF DEVOTION

HOURS OF DEVOTION

FANNY NEUDA'S BOOK OF PRAYERS
FOR JEWISH WOMEN

Edited and adapted into verse by

DINAH BERLAND

SCHOCKEN BOOKS, NEW YORK

Copyright © 2007 by Dinah Berland

All rights reserved. Published in the United States by Schocken Books, a division of Random House, Inc., New York, and in Canada
by Random House of Canada Limited, Toronto.

Schocken Books and colophon are registered trademarks
of Random House, Inc.

Much of the material in this book is translated from the original German work *Stunden der Andacht: Ein Gebet- und Erbauungs-Buch für Israels Frauen und Jungfrauen zur öffentlichen und häuslichen Andacht, sowie für alle Verhältnisse des weiblichen Lebens* by Fanny Neuda, first published by Wolf Pascheles, Prague, in 1855. The introduction from this work appears as the afterword to our edition. In addition, a brief excerpt is taken from the foreword by Wolf Pascheles, which appears in this edition. The remaining material in this book is adapted from the first English translation of this work, *Hours of Devotion: A Book of Prayers and Meditations for the Use of the Daughters of Israel, During Public Service and at Home, for all Conditions of Woman's Life*, translated by M[oritz] Mayer (New York: Hebrew Publishing Company, 1866). Most of the prayers and the afterword were translated from the German for this volume by Julia Watts Belser. Selected prayers, with changes, are from M[oritz] Mayer, trans., *Hours of Devotion: A Book of Prayers and Meditations for the Use of the Daughters of Israel, During Public Service and at Home, for All Conditions of Woman's Life* (New York: Hebrew Publishing Co., 1866). Fanny Neuda's preface translated by Steven Lindberg.

Library of Congress Cataloging-in-Publication Data
Neuda, Fanny, 1819–1894.
Hours of devotion : Fanny Neuda's book of prayers for Jewish women /
Fanny Neuda ; edited and adapted into verse by Dinah Berland.
p.   cm.
Original German edition appeared under the title, "Stunden der
Andacht," which was translated into English by M. Mayer (New York,
1866)—ECIP introduction.
Includes bibliographical references.
ISBN-13: 978-0-8052-4245-4
1. Jewish women—Prayer-books and devotions.   2. Judaism—
Prayer-books and devotions.   I. Berland, Dinah, 1941–   II. Title.
BM667.W6N4 2007
296.4'5082—dc22   2006038950

www.schocken.com

Printed in the United States of America

First Edition

2   4   6   8   9   7   5   3   1

In loving memory of my parents,
Jack A. Berland (1908–2003)
and Helen Berland (1914–1986)

For my children,
Adam, Jessica, and Rebecca,
and my grandchildren,
Hannah and Mia

לְדוֹר וָדוֹר

From generation to generation

CONTENTS

EDITOR'S PREFACE

If I had not fallen, I could not have arisen;
If I had not sat in darkness,
God would not have been a light for me.

—MIDRASH TEHILLIM
(Commentary on the Psalms), Chapter 22

From the women's gallery I gaze down at the vast sanctuary of the partially restored Loštice synagogue with its high vaulted ceilings and feel a sense of awe mixed with sadness. A plain blue curtain hangs against the eastern wall, where the altar once stood. On the main floor below, the men of the congregation once raised their voices in prayer; now, through broken windows, I hear only the call and response of birds.

This synagogue once held twenty-two Torah scrolls and was the center of a Jewish community that dates back to the sixteenth century. Today, in May 2006, the carved wooden doors are bolted shut, and not a single Jewish resident remains in Loštice; yet this small Moravian town has not forgotten its Jewish history. It remembers that more than 150 years ago, Fanny Neuda found peace and comfort here, as she wrote in her prayer "On Entering the Synagogue":

Merciful God, you are close to me everywhere,
But closest to me in this place.
Here I feel safe and secure in your protecting hand,
O Protector of All.
Here I feel shielded from life's uncertainties.
Here my soul willingly offers up its sacrifices,
And I gladly place my life at your disposal.
Here I disclose to you my innermost secrets and desires.

Fanny sat on this high balcony at the back of the synagogue with the women of her community, looking down toward the bimah, where her husband, Rabbi Abraham Neuda, led the congregation in prayer, courageously delivering his sermons in German so all could understand and learn. This is where Fanny later stood devastated at the age of thirty-five to say Kaddish for her husband, who died at forty-two. A few steps away, where the rabbi's living quarters once stood, is also where she composed her heartfelt prayers.

Fanny Neuda's collection, *Hours of Devotion*, was the first Jewish prayer book for all occasions written by a woman for women. A best-seller in the German language for more than a century, reprinted in twenty-eight editions between 1855 and 1918, translated into Yiddish in Europe and English in the United States, this remarkable book of prayers would bring solace to generations of women, and to me.

SEARCHING FOR A PRAYER

In the wake of a polarizing divorce, my first child and only son, Adam, then in his twenties, disappeared from my life for more than eleven years. All my attempts to contact him had failed. My friends and family provided support and advice, but one editorial client, the author Judith Orloff, M.D., offered the most radical suggestion of all. "There *is* something you can do," she said. "You can pray— it works."

I was a book editor for the J. Paul Getty Trust in Los Angeles. I was also a published poet and had previously worked as a freelance journalist, contributing regularly to the *Los Angeles Times,* among other newspapers and magazines. But this was not the kind of writing assignment I was used to. What sort of prayer could I possibly compose that would be neither too selfish nor too weak? How could I ever find words strong and loving enough to heal the painful rift between us?

Then one day, as I was browsing in Sam Johnson's Book Shop around the corner from my house, I noticed a slim, well-worn volume tucked between larger tomes in the Judaica section. The spine was mysteriously blank. Out of curiosity, I plucked it off the shelf and discovered *Hours of Devotion: A Book of Prayers and Meditations for the Use of the Daughters of Israel, During Public Service and at Home, for All Conditions of Woman's Life,* translated by M. Mayer "from the German *Stunden der Andacht*" (New York, 1866). The author's name was notably absent.

As I scanned the table of contents—skimming past the morning and evening prayers, prayers for each day of the week, for the Sabbath, the New Moon, and the Jewish holidays—I was captivated by the many prayers written especially for women. There were personal prayers for a bride, for a woman about to give birth, for mothers with grown children, for widows. In addition were special prayers that could be used by men as well as women and by people of any faith—for travel, for patience and strength, for healing, for thanksgiving, and for loss.

Then I saw the title "A Mother's Prayer Whose Child Is Abroad."[1] I was stunned to discover that someone had actually written a prayer for a woman whose child was absent from her life, a woman like me. As I began to read the heartfelt pleas of a mother asking God to watch over her child when she could not, to "lead him safely over every rock and thorn in his path," to "grant him strength and calm"—I felt, at last, that someone understood both my pain and my hope. The last lines contained the message I had been seeking:

> O Parent of All, hear my fervent prayer
> And bring my child back to me
> At the right time, full of joy and the vigor of life,
> To be the pride and delight of my heart,
> A blessing to all, and pleasing in your sight,
> My God and Sovereign. Amen.

I bought the book and began to read that prayer often—then the prayers for morning and evening, and then the days of the week. Each time I dipped into this slender volume, I felt comforted. Almost immediately I began to imagine the possibility of updating it for a modern-day audience.

Then a chain of amazing events began to unfold. I was preparing for my father's ninetieth birthday party to be held in my hometown of Milwaukee, Wisconsin, by producing a limited-edition oral history I had conducted with my father to present as a gift to our family. My father had often said he wanted the words *l'dor va-dor* (from generation to generation) inscribed on his tombstone, and since my initial purpose in interviewing him was to discover what values he wanted to pass down, I also decided to use this as the title of his birthday booklet. In the process of searching through family photographs to illustrate the text, I came across pictures of my son as a child and was flooded with feelings of love and sorrow. I recalled how close Adam had been to his grandfather. What a joy it would be for my father to see him, or even to hear from him again. This led to what seemed an impossible idea at the time: What if I were to send Adam an invitation to the party? If he did nothing more than send a birthday card, it would bring his grandfather such happiness. When I asked a few trusted family members what they thought of the idea, each one advised me not to do it, that it would only bring me more disappointment and pain.

Then came Rosh Hashanah, the Jewish New Year, a time for reflection and change. I had married a non-Jewish man and had not been attending synagogue regularly, but High Holiday services were a given, so we decided to try Leo Baeck Temple, a Reform congregation we had visited occasionally. On the eve of the holiday, Rabbi Emily Feigenson gave a sermon on signs from God. "You know when it's time to reach out to someone who has hurt you," she said. "The sign is a broken heart." All at once I heard myself sob out loud and felt the tears streaming down my cheeks. I knew I had to invite Adam to the party. The next day I picked up one of the invitations, illustrated with a sepia-tone photograph of my father at age thirteen, holding a violin in his lap—his bar mitzvah portrait. I addressed the envelope, walked to the corner mailbox, and dropped it in. I felt as if I were tossing a stone into the ocean, with no expectation whatsoever of what might become of it, and doing this gave me a sense of great freedom. That day I also decided to join the temple.

Two weeks later a representative from the congregation was due to arrive at our house for a membership interview. I had just come home from the farmer's market, and my arms were filled with gladiolas. The phone rang, I put down the flowers, and a voice at the other end said, "Hello. This is going to come as a big surprise to you. This is your son, Adam." I could hardly believe my ears.

"I received your invitation," the voice at the other end said, "and I'm calling to let you know that I'm coming."

Not knowing if he would hang up immediately, not knowing if this was even really my son, whose voice I hadn't heard in more than a decade, all I could say was, "I have to tell you—this is an answer to a prayer."

That was the beginning of a new and beautiful chapter in our relationship, one that is even more precious to us than it might have been, perhaps, because of the years we missed. What I didn't understand at the time but have now come to realize through the process of working on this book is that the very act of sending that invitation was a form of prayer—that sometimes we can pray without even knowing it. We can pray with our hearts alone. Fanny's humble little book, with its fervent expressions of true feeling, had given me the courage to do what I needed to do. It had begun to help me heal.

Soon after this life-altering experience, I began to think more seriously about how wonderful it would be if others could have access to this extraordinary book so they, too, might be comforted and find an avenue toward personal prayer. For five years the idea of updating *Hours of Devotion* for a contemporary audience remained just that. Meanwhile, my life began to move in unexpected directions, leading me further into Jewish study and practice. Without being fully conscious of it, I was preparing for the work I needed to do.

GOD IN THE ROOM

I was a spiritual child, as perhaps all young children are. My parents, who were active in our Reform congregation in Milwaukee, enrolled me in religious school at an early age and frequently took me to services. I loved sitting in the large vaulted sanctuary of Temple Emanu-El B'ne Jeshurun with its plush burgundy-velvet seats, staring up at the paintings of Abraham and Sarah, Moses, and Joseph on the domed ceiling above and wondering how Isaac must have felt when his father took him up the mountain and what Joseph's coat of many colors must have looked like. When I was about seven years old, my mother helped me compose my own bedtime prayer, which we would recite together each night:

> God bless my mother, my father,
> My sister, my brother, all my relatives,
> My country, my friends, and myself.
> May we all live healthy, happy, and together. Amen.

After my mother turned out the lights, I would often sit up in bed in the dark and think about God. When I did this, I would sometimes feel a tingling sensation at the very top of my head, which gave me a wonderful feeling of happiness and calm. I came to believe that God was not a bearded old man gazing down from some distant, heavenly throne, like in my illustrated Bible, but rather very close, right there in my room.

When I was about nine or ten years old, my grandfather tried to teach me Kabbalah. Grandpa Berland was a scholar from Kiev and a man of great kindness and humility. As the story goes, he had narrowly escaped being forcibly conscripted into the czar's army. No one knows exactly what my grandmother, then pregnant with my Aunt Sophia, told the soldiers who pounded at the door, but that night they packed what they could carry and fled Ukraine with their three-year-old daughter, my Aunt Fanny, and one small diamond sewn inside a coat.

On one memorable occasion during my early childhood, my father and grandfather spent all evening after our Passover Seder arguing about how God had actually parted the Red Sea. My father, an attorney and a man of logic, argued that it must have been the result of an unusual meteorological event—a freak storm combined with unusually low tides, or some other occurrence with a rational explanation. But my grandfather would have none of that. "It was a miracle," he calmly insisted again and again, "a miracle from God." He had, after all, experienced miracles of his own.

One day my grandfather invited me to sit down with him at the table. He spread out a piece of paper containing the Hebrew alphabet. "These letters are also numbers," he began, "and they can be arranged and rearranged to make everything in the universe." Though I didn't understand much of what he was trying to teach me, I have never forgotten the impact of those lessons, which I sensed held a knowledge that was both mysterious and profound. By introducing me to the secrets of mystical Judaism, my grandfather made me feel very special and, perhaps unknowingly, ignited a spark that would ultimately illuminate the spiritual direction of my life.

I had the honor of being the first girl trained at my temple to become a bat mitzvah (literally, daughter of the commandments). When that long-awaited morning arrived, I entered the temple in my new pink piqué dress and white patent-leather shoes, stepped up to the bimah with as much courage as I could muster, and read from the Torah before a congregation filled with family and friends. After completing my reading and then delivering the speech my father had largely written for me, I found myself standing in front of the rabbi, my eyes at about the level of his tie clip. As Rabbi Herbert A. Friedman—a tall, handsome man with a sonorous voice—placed his hands lightly above my head to bestow the priestly blessing, I felt something I had never felt before and had no words for. It was a sense of pure, absolute love. I was deeply moved but also confused. No one had ever taught me about the heart's connection to the divine, and I had no context for this powerful feeling of exaltation. Later, as the guests were just beginning to arrive for the reception at our home, I pulled my mother aside and asked her with troubled intensity, "Mother, do you think the rabbi was sincere?" No doubt finding my innocent bewilderment amusing, and perhaps not knowing how to explain an experience to me that she had never had, she began to laugh and immediately repeated my words to other family members. I felt keenly embarrassed and never again asked such a question.

FROM SOURCE TO SOURCE

As an adult, my circuitous spiritual path—punctuated by bouts of struggle and loss—led me on a long quest, often far from Judaism, to try to recapture the sense of acceptance, love, and communion with God that I had glimpsed as a child. In the 1970s, I dabbled in Buddhism, used a book to teach myself to meditate, and in the early 1980s became involved in the Hindu spiritual practice of Siddha Yoga with the guru Swami Muktananda.

At the height of my involvement in Siddha Yoga, I meditated daily, bought a silk sari, burned Blue Pearl incense, and would habitually wake up before dawn—although I had never been an early riser—to drive five miles to the ashram for the morning chant to the guru, which was accompanied by the haunting rhythms of sitar and tabla. My meditation experience was so blissful that at first I thought someone must be pumping marijuana into the air-conditioning system. I became so entranced by the floating sensation I felt during deep meditation that I even lost my lifelong fear of swimming. Then one evening while standing in line, waiting to kneel at the guru's feet and offer him a flower in exchange for a swat on the head from his peacock feather, I woke up to the fact that bowing down to another human being was definitely "not Jewish." I finally stopped attending, though I did continue to meditate for years, if only sporadically. Ultimately, I drifted back to my Reform habit of three-times-a-year Judaism, attending services for the High Holidays, and celebrating Passover and Hanukkah.

Then in early 2001 a memo came across my desk that would change my life utterly. The Getty Trust informed all vested employees that they could apply for a "Study and Renewal Leave"—three months of paid leave, with benefits and a travel allowance, to study or pursue a project anywhere in the world. I had been longing for a stretch of time and the freedom to work on my own poetry and decided to apply for a self-styled writing retreat in San Miguel de Allende, a beautiful, historic town in central Mexico, where my husband and I had celebrated our tenth wedding anniversary the year before. I set off on my two-month sojourn with a mixture of excitement and anxiety, sensing that the period of solitude I had chosen, far from everything and everyone familiar in my life, would be a turning point in ways I could not then imagine.

In the suitcase I reserved for books, I packed (along with several volumes of poetry, astronomy, physics, birdwatching, and a music dictionary) Rabbi David Cooper's inspiring book *God Is a Verb* and Rodger Kamenetz's *The Jew in the Lotus*,[2] a book my cousin Mel's wife, Ruth, had plucked off her daughter-in-law's bookshelf and spontaneously thrust into my hands for no apparent reason during a recent family reunion. "Here. I think you'll like this book," she said. I didn't know at the time that Cooper had studied with Rabbi Zalman Schachter-Shalomi, one of the Jewish leaders featured in Kamenetz's book, nor that "Reb Zalman" had inspired and guided the Jewish Renewal movement, to which I would soon be introduced.

Since I knew no one in San Miguel and was planning to be in town for Rosh Hashanah, I decided to join the weekly Torah study group there. On my first visit the leader handed me a flyer stating that this was "a Jewish Renewal community," which I later learned meant an inclusive, egalitarian approach to Judaism that brings the spiritual traditions of Kabbalah, contemplative practice, and Hasidic ritual into a contemporary context.

One Sabbath morning, a woman in the study group read an e-mail commentary on that week's Torah portion that was unlike any Jewish teaching I'd ever heard before. When I asked who wrote it, she told me it was by Rami Shapiro, a rabbi who had just moved from Florida to Los Angeles— where I lived—to lead an organization called Metivta, a Center for Contemplative Judaism, founded by Rabbi Jonathan Omer-Man, another of the progressive rabbis featured in *The Jew in the Lotus*. The following week the woman returned with one of Rabbi Rami's books, *Minyan: Ten Principles for Living a Life of Integrity.*[3] The first principle was "Meditate." Could there really be such a thing as Jewish meditation? I was thrilled to discover that there was and that it was remarkably similar to the meditation I had been practicing in Siddha Yoga, except using Jewish prayer as the mantra—especially the Shema, the central prayer of Judaism, affirming the oneness of God. How wonderful was that? From that day on, I began meditating daily, this time within my own religious tradition.

But my joy didn't last long. I returned home to national and personal devastation. The terrorist attacks of September 11 had just shaken the world and, though I had refused to see it coming, my marriage soon imploded as well. I had returned to a traumatized world, I was inconsolable, and I needed spiritual guidance more than ever. I looked up Metivta's address, only to discover that I had been driving right past it on my way home from work every workday for more than two years. I began attending the weekly meditation and Torah study sessions there, at first mainly as a respite from the pain. I was becoming quite skilled at driving while crying.

One night a scholar by the name of Ronnie Serr came to teach. In presenting the story of Joseph being sold into slavery, the Torah portion for the week, he conveyed a powerful teaching from the Ba'al Shem Tov, a five-step process from suffering to thanksgiving, with prayer at its center. The first step is suffering, which does not need to be sought, since it comes to us all; second is the acceptance of suffering, which is a practice of awareness; third is the act of prayer, calling out to God for help; fourth is the gift of redemption, which comes as a direct result of prayer; and fifth is thanksgiving, which springs naturally from the experience of being heard and received.

As far removed as I was then from being able to accept my suffering as a step toward anything—I just wanted the pain to go away—the very thought struck me to the core. I approached Ronnie after class to tell him how much his teaching had meant to me because I was going through a period of so much suffering. He listened to me, looked deep into my eyes, and with great compassion said, "The world is for you." In that moment I knew I had found my teacher.

On the way home, driving with tears streaming down my face, I could feel my brokenness as though my pain were an entity in itself. I was keenly aware of my suffering and felt helpless to stop it. So I cried out loud to God, pleading for help with every sob, asking to be relieved of this terrible sorrow. Then, instantaneously, just as I was reaching the crest of a hill, a sensation of calm descended on me like a blanket of light. My sobbing stopped, and all at once I felt as peaceful as if I had been meditating for hours. I was so transformed by this sudden emotional shift that I could do nothing but laugh in thanksgiving, amazed and grateful that prayer could really work in this way, even for a minute, even for a second. Although it had not been my conscious intention, I had clearly absorbed Ronnie's teaching and put it into action. Something profound had happened to me simply by acknowledging the truth of my soul and asking God for help.

FROM GENERATION TO GENERATION

Since that night I've had many more opportunities to learn the transformative power of personal prayer. Beginning in early 2002, I began attending Ronnie's Shir HaShirim (Song of Songs) class, a private study group that has grown into an intimate spiritual community. When my father died on Thanksgiving Day 2003, one day before his ninety-fifth birthday, Ronnie invited me to share stories of his life with the group. I presented the illustrated booklet I'd produced, *L'Dor Va-Dor: From Generation to Generation*, the project that had led to my son's return. Doing so made me realize that the time had come to begin work on that nineteenth-century Jewish prayer book for women I'd shelved away years before. I would launch this endeavor as a tribute to my father's memory.

I still had no idea about the origin of *Hours of Devotion*, who might have written it, or how popular it had been. So I turned to bibliographic researcher Valerie Greathouse, a longtime Getty colleague, to do some sleuthing for me. A few days later, I opened my e-mail, and, like words rising to the surface inside a black oracle ball, a name popped up on my computer screen: Fanny Neuda (née Schmiedl), 1819–1894. Just as I'd hoped and imagined, the author was a woman.

Once I learned her name, I was able to discover that Fanny Neuda was born on March 6, 1819, in the Moravian town of Ivančice (then Eibenschutz, Austria) and had married Rabbi Abraham Neuda (1812–1854) of Loštice (then Loschitz, Austria),[4] where she was living in 1855, when her book was published. When I did an initial Internet search for this town, the first site that came up was that of Respect and Tolerance, an independent foundation in Loštice, Czech Republic, dedicated to documenting and preserving the Jewish history of that area.[5] There I learned that the earliest record of Jewish presence in Loštice was from 1544; that by 1849, when Fanny and her family lived there, the Jewish community represented 17 percent of the total population, living in mutual cooperation with its Christian neighbors; that by 1942 the last remaining Jewish residents were rounded up and taken to concentration camps, most to their deaths; and that the town doesn't have a single Jewish resident today.

Exploring further, I found a vivid painting by Judith Joseph, *Memorial for Jewish Victims of the Holocaust, Loštice, Czech Republic*, 2005,[6] which contains the following text in large Hebrew letters: "You must do the same with your brother's donkey, his garment, or anything else your brother loses and you find: You must not ignore it" (Deut. 22:3). The personal message I took from this verse was that since I had found Fanny Neuda's book of prayers—or, in another sense, it had found me—I had a sacred duty to bring it back to life.

On learning that Judith Joseph was educated in Wisconsin and had exhibited her work in Milwaukee, my hometown, I decided to contact her. My late mother, Helen Berland, was also a Wisconsin artist, and I was curious to find out if Judith may have known of my mother and also what Judith's connection to Loštice might be. Not only did she recall my mother's work, but their paintings had hung together in a 1994 exhibition celebrating the sesquicentennial of Jewish presence in Wisconsin at the Haggerty Museum of Art at Marquette University. How likely was it that I would stumble across a person connected both to my own home and to Fanny's, and both through links to Jewish history? The synchronicities connected with this project were beginning to feel like a series of little miracles. But the connection between Judith's current home in a Chicago suburb and that small town in the Czech Republic runs even deeper.

Following World War II, a Torah scroll from Loštice—

among the more than 1,500 scrolls that were confiscated by the Nazis from Bohemia and Moravia and later salvaged and redistributed to Jewish congregations around the world— had made its way to Congregation Hakafa in Glencoe, Illinois. Stanton Canter, an American doctor who first visited Loštice in 2000, was so deeply moved by his experience there that he joined with Czech conservator Luděk Štipl to establish the Respect and Tolerance foundation. Dr. Canter then succeeded in locating the Loštice Torah that was being cared for by the Hakafa congregation, thus initiating the process that would bring the scroll back to the Czech Republic for the first Torah reading in the old Loštice synagogue since World War II.[7] Judith Joseph was part of that delegation and created her Loštice memorial painting for the occasion. Also, since the trip coincided with the week of her own bat mitzvah Torah portion, Judith was invited to read from the historic scroll during the Sabbath service.

Honoring the nearly four centuries of peaceful relationship between the Christian and Jewish populations in Loštice, the Respect and Tolerance foundation, under the direction of Luděk Štipl, has partially restored the Loštice synagogue, where Fanny's husband and his father before him served as rabbis, and has documented the more than six hundred tombstones in the old Jewish cemetery nearby.[8] There, on a graceful hillside strewn with wildflowers and sheltered by linden trees, the tombstones, all inscribed with Hebrew letters, tilt and touch, "supporting each other like family," as Stanton Canter puts it. Under low tree limbs at the crest of the hill, the large headstone bearing Abraham Neuda's name can still be found, now lying nearly flat against the ground.

A LIFE OF PRAYER

Fanny Neuda was born into a rabbinical family on both her mother's and her father's side. Her maternal grandfather,

Rabbi Moses haKohen Karpeles (1765–1837), was, as his name indicates, from the priestly tribe of Kohanim (Cohens). He and his wife, Titl Grünbaum Karpeles, raised three sons and a daughter. All the sons became rabbis, and the daughter, Nechoma Karpeles, married Rabbi Juda Schmiedl (1776–1855), Fanny's father.[9] Thus, Fanny grew up steeped in religious study and worship. In a very real sense, prayer was her birthright.

By the time she was two years old, Fanny's family had moved to nearby Prostějov (then Prossnitz), a flourishing center of talmudic study and home to her grandfather Moses.[10] It was there that Fanny's brother, Adolf Schmiedl (1821–1913), was born. Like his father, grandfather, and uncles before him, Adolf became a rabbi. He officiated in Prostějov from 1853 to 1869, briefly in Loštice after Abraham's death, and eventually assumed a prominent rabbinical post in Vienna. Along with Abraham Neuda, Adolf Schmiedl is counted among the first generation of "modern" rabbis in Moravia.[11] A widely published Talmudic scholar and religious philosopher, he wrote on the relationship of Judaism and Christianity, Arabic-Jewish philosophy, and a range of esoteric subjects, including angelology and reincarnation.

Fanny lived in heady and often contentious times. For generations, Moravian Jews had been granted only very restricted legal rights to property, education, and the types of businesses they could own. They suffered under laws that regulated even the number of men per town who were permitted to marry, thus effectively limiting the Jewish population. The "enlightened" Hapsburg emperor, Joseph II (1741–1790), began stripping away many of these discriminatory laws. His 1781 Edict of Toleration made education accessible to all, opened the universities to Jews, and allowed for their widespread integration into the general population. Local schools and institutions opened their doors to Jewish enrollment, and the government encouraged Jewish communities to establish their own schools to instruct students in a range of subjects. All the students were taught in German, which soon replaced Yiddish as the common language for Jews throughout Bohemia and Moravia.

Yet some restrictions to Jewish housing, employment, and even the number of Jews who could marry still persisted. After the Revolution of 1848, those limits were finally relaxed, and the new emperor, Franz Joseph I (1830–1916), championed full civil rights for all citizens, permitting Jews to reside in all areas of Moravia and granting them equality with Christians under the law. Franz Joseph thus became a beloved figure among the Jewish people. Fanny's original (1855) "Prayer for the Leaders of Our Country" blesses him by name, along with the first Queen Elizabeth.[12] As the Enlightenment began to spread through Europe in the mid-eighteenth century, Jews began to leave the ghettos to which they had largely been confined and enjoy more social and cultural freedoms. This led to the emergence of the Haskalah, or Jewish Enlightenment, which emphasized the era's broad cultural values of rationalism and justice and brought about many educational advances, including the education of women.

The Haskalah gave rise to the Reform movement of early-nineteenth-century Germany, a movement that aimed to modernize Jewish practice, stem the loss of Jews to secular nationalism, and gain acceptability for Jewry within the larger European society. At first the reformers introduced relatively modest changes in religious services, such as allowing organ music and sermons delivered in the common language—which, in Moravia at the time, was German. It wasn't long, however, before various rabbinical assemblies had formed and were advocating far more extreme changes, such as moving the Sabbath to Sunday and eliminating the study of Hebrew. Bitter debates arose regarding nearly every rite and ritual, including dietary laws, circumcision, and the validity of the Talmud. At one point, Orthodox leaders from Moravia, Bohemia, Germany, and Hungary joined forces to condemn all aspects of the Reform movement, fearing the unraveling of the very fabric of Judaism itself.[13]

Voices of moderation also existed, however, most notably that of Isaac Noah Mannheimer (1793–1865), a prominent Vienna preacher, born in Copenhagen, who forged a "middle road" approach and who would ultimately play a significant role in Abraham Neuda's life. Mannheimer persuasively argued for the inspirational value of delivering sermons in the vernacular and that this could be done without losing the essential aspects of religious liturgy and ritual, including the use of Hebrew as the language of worship.[14] His oratorical gifts and widely published views helped prevent a split in the Jewish community at the time and have had far-reaching affects on religious observance, in all denominations, to this day.

Prostějov, where Fanny most likely spent her formative years, was then the center of the Reform movement in Moravia. It is evident from the quotations and allusions that punctuate her prayers that she was educated in both secular and Judaic studies. Her rich background in the German classics and philosophy were made possible not only by virtue of her privileged upbringing but also by the open spirit of the Enlightenment.

Her prayer "On the First Days of Sukkot" makes poignantly clear the sense of freedom and security she felt living in Moravia in the 1850s, as if such peace and social acceptance could last forever. Addressing God, she writes:

> Your compassion has held us and carried us
> Through storm and flood, over every abyss
> That has threatened to devour us.
> And now, after generations of wandering,
> You have allowed us to taste the sweetness of home.
> Thanks to you, we have found a homeland—

A beautiful, wonderful country
That recognizes us as its children.

It was within this liberal and increasingly secularized environment that Fanny Neuda produced an essay on the importance of providing a religious education to young women. Published as an introduction to the first edition of her prayer book and as an afterword to all later German editions, "Ein Wort an die edlen Mütter und Frauen in Israel" (A Word to the Noble Mothers and Women of Israel), strongly encourages Jewish mothers to guide their daughters toward a "nobility of feeling and deeply felt religiosity," which are "a woman's highest ornaments."[15]

The opening paragraphs of her essay, in which she lauds the domestic roles of women, may seem from today's perspective to be at odds with the forward-thinking attitude toward women's religious education she expresses later; but, taken in the context of Fanny's time and place, both spring from the same source: the desire to restore dignity and religious fulfillment to Jewish women caught between two worlds. Free to learn foreign languages and read the great secular literature of their day—as their pious brothers were not—Jewish young women in mid-nineteenth-century Eastern Europe were exposed to a worldly culture they could never fully enter, even as they were denied the religious education afforded to men. The results were that many Jewish women intermarried and attempted to assimilate, while others married Jewish men and embarked on family life with only a routine understanding of the tradition they practiced.

Having had the opportunity to pursue Jewish study within her own rabbinical family, and having married a rabbi with whom, as she suggests in her preface, she shared a rich spiritual life, Fanny must have sorely lamented this situation. Thus she makes a passionate plea for honoring wives and mothers as transmitters of knowledge and values and for instilling in young women a deeper appreciation of their own religious heritage—a heritage that was, and has always been, inseparable from the Hebrew language.[16]

> For why should our daughters, who invest such time and energy learning to play the piano and to sing opera, who study languages that are fashionable and *en vogue* today, not also devote an hour each day to the learning of our holy tongue, the noble mother of all languages, the language that is the key to those treasures of the heart and mind that God set down in his Book, which we so appropriately call "the book of books"? Shouldn't they dedicate a small portion of their time to learning *the language* that remains the bond uniting all members of the Jewish people scattered throughout all the countries of the world?

Learning Hebrew and acquiring a quality religious education would not only benefit the young woman herself, she asserts, but would also one day serve as "a real blessing for her home and for the world, for the past and for the future." The blessing here is not only the ability to transmit religious knowledge but also to inspire spiritual awareness. For just as the beauty and sincerity of Fanny Neuda's prayers transcend all considerations of time and culture, so her essay emphasizes *"the ennobling of the heart, the development and strengthening of religious feeling"* above all else.[17]

Through the lens of history—a history characterized by spasms of persecution, forced conversion, and even assimilation by choice—baking (or just serving) challah and lighting Sabbath candles are not trivial rituals; they are nothing less than tools for a people's survival. Yet Fanny is asking for more than domestic ritual; she is asking that Jewish mothers, along with the community at large, make a commitment to educating their daughters in Judaism and to leading them by example.

Fanny's own domestic life began in storybook fashion. Following family tradition, she married a rabbi from a rabbinical family, and a Cohen as well.[18] Abraham was one of the first "progressive" rabbis in Moravia, a scholar and a widely published writer on Talmud and Moravian Jewish history with a broad secular as well as a religious education. In December 1835, on the death of his father, Rabbi Aaron Moses Neuda (1761–1835) of Loštice, the community elected Abraham as his successor. In the climate of growing reform and rising animosity between conservative and liberal Jewish leadership, the chief rabbi of Moravia vehemently opposed Abraham's election, arguing that the young rabbi "preached in German and [had] acquired too much secular education."[19] The Neudas' life thus changed dramatically, as they were caught up in a drawn-out legal battle that attracted widespread attention, pitting advocates for reform against those who were staunchly opposed to it. For six long years Abraham and Fanny found themselves in the eye of a very public storm. The proceedings finally terminated in Abraham's favor but only after he had passed an examination before a committee consisting of a board of rabbis along with a Catholic priest. Abraham's defender in this trial was none other than Isaac Mannheimer, author of the Viennese rite.[20]

Abraham Neuda ultimately served for nearly two decades as rabbi of Loštice, but the stress presumably took a serious toll on his health, as Fanny implies in her preface (which follows here, for the first time in English). He died in 1854 at the age of forty-two, leaving Fanny a widow at only thirty-five, with three sons under the age of twelve. What was she to do? As her writings show, Fanny was a woman of not only great humility but also great faith and strength. In her preface she writes that she did not compose her prayers for publication but rather out of a profound desire to speak to God. She ultimately decided to publish her book "in living memory" of her husband: "Most of these prayers are the outpourings of my heart associated with events I experienced at his side, with him and through him."[21] These events were not always pleasant, yet her prayers transcend all conflict, all animosity. As she eloquently writes in her prayer for Wednesday,

> [Y]ou send us your comforting, heavenly light
> When nights of adversity and misfortune
> Darken our souls.
> When worries and troubles cloud our lives,
> You will let the sun of your holy grace and mercy
> Shine above us once more.
> When devastating fortunes threaten to devour us,
> You will unfurl evening's shadow.

Relying on her faith, her family, and her community, Fanny found the courage to carry on and to complete the work she was meant to do. She soon gained the support of a notable contemporary, Baroness Louise von Rothschild (1820–1894), wife of M. Carl von Rothschild of Frankfurt, the woman to whom all the early German editions of Fanny's book are dedicated, to help sponsor the publication of her work. In 1855, three publishers (in Prague, Leipzig, and Frankfurt) brought out the first edition of Fanny Neuda's *Hours of Devotion*.[22]

Much remains to be discovered about Fanny's life after her husband's death, yet some tantalizing clues have begun to emerge from research in the Czech Republic and Austria, conducted in large part by the Respect and Tolerance foundation. According to the Loštice census record of 1857, Fanny was still living at the Loštice synagogue address at that time, along with her three sons, and sharing the rabbi's apartments with Rabbi Elias Karpeles, her first cousin.[23] Fanny's name does not appear in the town's census of 1869, however, indicating that she moved sometime after 1857. The trail picks up again in 1880 in Vienna, where a list of "foreigners" (i.e., new residents) names Fanny Neuda as "living alone at Grosse Mohrengasse no. 2," a street that still exists.[24] Her brother, Adolf, was then serving as a rabbi in Vienna, and Fanny—at age sixty-one, with her children now grown—evidently joined him there.

Although further details of Fanny's life remain a mystery, the life of her prayer book is no secret. It was a popular success that would extend well into the next century. Fanny also published two collections of stories for children in 1867 and 1876,[25] but it was *Hours of Devotion* that brought her the most acclaim. Whether by virtue of her writing career or through other means, Fanny had enough resources later in life to travel to the still-popular spa town of Merano, Italy (then Meran, Austria), the "jewel of the Tyrol" in the Austrian-Italian Alps, where she died on April 16, 1894, at the age of seventy-five. The original version of her prayer book remained in print another twenty-four years, continuing through a twenty-eighth edition, published in 1918 (or later).

CALLING OUT TO GOD

Though Fanny Neuda's work is distinctive, calling out to God in a consistent tone of reverence, humility, and trust, it also gives voice to women in many different life situations—from young woman to mother, from bride to widow, from poverty-stricken to the prosperous. Her prayers were not written in a vacuum. They grew out of a popular genre of personal, devotional prayers for women, initially written primarily in Yiddish, called *tkhines* (supplications), that had been produced in Europe since the sixteenth century.[26] *Tkhines* were prayers, first published in Yiddish and later in German, mainly for the use of Ashkenazic Jewish women, who were generally not taught Hebrew but who wanted to observe the rabbinic requirement to pray to God at least once a day. In both Eastern and Western Europe, the demand was high for *tkhine* collections through the early twentieth century. These books were typically compiled from various sources, especially the Psalms, which were considered to be the most appropriate reading material for Jewish women.

Collections of *tkhines* did not usually indicate their authors' identities, though most are thought to have been written and/or compiled by men, commonly under female pseudonyms or with first initials only, to make them more appealing to their primarily female audience.[27] This probably explains why the title page of the first English edition of *Hours of Devotion* (1866) gives the name "M. Mayer" rather than the full name and title of its translator, Rabbi Moritz Mayer (1821–1867), a German-born lawyer and rabbi who emigrated to the United States in 1848. Mayer first lived in New York and then, from 1852 to 1859, served as rabbi at Kahal Kadosh Beth Elohim in Charleston, South Carolina, the first congregation in the United States to adopt Reform Judaism. Mayer finally returned to New York, where he wrote for the Jewish press and also translated a number of German texts into English. *Hours of Devotion*, published a year before his death, was likely his last and certainly his most significant work.[28]

Fanny was familiar with many of the prayer books for women on the market in her day and alludes to their mostly male authorship. As she writes in her preface, "We already possess some excellent writings in this genre—devotional books for women, penned by men." The structure as well as the subject matter of Fanny's volume of prayers refer back at least two centuries to the *Seyder Tkhines*, a model Yiddish prayer book for women published between 1648 and 1723.[29] By the mid-1800s, there were numerous examples of such books on the market in Europe. Yet when the first edition of *Hours of Devotion* appeared in 1855, written in German, it was immediately exceptional, not only for its high level of scholarship, emotional depth, wisdom, and poetic voice but also for its female authorship.[30] Wolf Pascheles, the Prague publisher of that first edition, writes in his foreword, "For the first time, a respected woman has composed a prayer book for weekdays, festivals, and fast days that speaks to all aspects of a woman's life."[31] According to German scholar Bettina Kratz-Ritter, *Hours of Devotion* was considered "the authoritative women's prayer book of its time," in large part because it was "the first of this genre written by a woman for women."[32] In an article focusing on Fanny Neuda's representation of women, Kratz-Ritter notes, referring to the German editions, that Fanny's volume was "the women's prayer book that was and has remained a classic throughout the second half of the nineteenth century and into our own," primarily due to its female authorship.[33]

In the preface to *Hours of Devotion*, Fanny affirms the advantage of a female perspective for such books: "A man, however learned and great he may be, cannot capture the essential quality of a woman's experience," whereas a woman "need only gaze into her own heart to read the hearts of her sisters." She could have known only vicariously the suffering of some of her sisters, such as that of an orphan, a childless wife, or a mother with daughters; but the pain of others, such as a widow with young children, or a wife mourning the death of her husband, she would have known only too well.

I was moved to find that just as Fanny had published her prayers to honor the memory of her late husband, so I had ultimately begun working on this project soon after the loss of my father. I also learned that I was not the first to produce a revised edition of this book. In 1936, Martha Wertheimer released an edited version of *Hours of Devotion* in modern German type.[34] Recounting the popularity of the original text, Wertheimer writes in her preface:

Fanny Neuda's *Hours of Devotion* was always in the hands of our grandmothers and mothers when, alongside the

Hebrew prayers of the *tefillah* [formal prayer], they turned to God in their own language when they gave thanks or sought solace on occasions of joy or trouble. Grandmothers and mothers also gave the book to their granddaughters and daughters. . . . It still retains the qualities that accounted for its popularity among Jewish women in Germany: its deep piety, childlike trust, a reverent admiration of all creation, kindness of heart, and a living and lived relationship to Jewish customs, festivals, and commandments.[35]

Wertheimer's edition was published in Frankfurt during the rise of the Third Reich. It's a wonder that any copies managed to survive Nazi Germany, but some clearly did. The inscription on the one I own indicates that it was given as a gift in 1938. The original owners of Fanny's cherished little prayer book must have carefully safeguarded them, tucking them into their belongings along with family photos as they escaped persecution to safer corners of Europe, to Israel, and abroad to the Americas and other distant lands.[36]

Just when I thought the 1936 version was the end of the story, I noticed some dates even more recent cropping up in the bibliographic record, from the 1950s and even 1960s. Incredibly, the Wertheimer edition of *Hours of Devotion* had resurfaced in Basel, Switzerland, after World War II and remained in print until 1968. Today the remaining copies of Fanny Neuda's prayer book for women, now long out of print, reflect the story of the Diaspora itself—dispersed into libraries and private collections across the globe. In 1942, according to Ismar Schorsch's moving account, his aunt Helene Rothschild carried her 1873 German copy of *Hours of Devotion* into the "model" concentration camp at Terezín (Theresienstadt). Helene survived, as did the book, and Schorsch still keeps this volume among his most treasured possessions.[37]

Several prayers from *Hours of Devotion* have appeared in

contemporary anthologies of Jewish women's literature in German, English, and most recently in Hebrew.[38] In *Four Centuries of Jewish Women's Spirituality*, coeditor Ellen M. Umansky notes that when she had occasion to mention Fanny's prayer book to synagogue groups across the United States, many older Jewish women from Germany would come forward to tell her that they had received the book as a gift from their mothers, "many on their wedding day." Some told her that "every Jewish woman in [early-twentieth-century] Germany owned the book." Some of these early copies were passed from hand to hand during World War II, she reports, and one had been given to the owner's mother by another woman when they were both in hiding.[39]

LEARNING TO WORSHIP

When I first began to adapt these prayers for a twenty-first-century audience, my initial intention was simply to lightly edit and personalize Mayer's translation by converting the address of "Thee" and "Thou" to "you," removing gender-specific references to God, reorganizing some of the entries and chapter divisions, and editing for contemporary syntax and clarity. After I'd had the opportunity to examine several of the early German editions, which include the author's preface, her essay, the full complement of prayers, and verses from the Bible and other sources that she used as epigraphs, I decided to reinstate a large part of the missing material and also to learn as much about Fanny's life and work as possible. I would strive not only to bring a book from another century into the present but also to carry with it some of the content and information that had never before been available to readers of English.

Mayer's translation, representing 67 of the 117 prayers in the German original, remained in print until around 1900.[40] After the book had been accepted for publication, I started looking for a translator from the German, preferably a woman with some knowledge of Jewish literature. My teacher, Ronnie Serr, recommended the ideal person: Julia Watts Belser, a rabbinical student at the Academy for Jewish Religion in Los Angeles and a doctoral candidate in Jewish folklore and gender studies at the University of California at Berkeley with fluent command of German. One of the first tasks I asked Julia to undertake was a verification of Mayer's 1866 translation against the German. To my dismay I learned that less than half of the prayers corresponded with Fanny's writing. Many of them were titled correctly but the text was different, others lacked significant chunks of material, and a few of Mayer's prayers didn't appear in the original German at all.[41] Those that were true to Fanny's work, however, were quite lyrical as well as accurate.

Next, I selected a group of prayers for retranslation from the Mayer book and also about thirty others from the original German that did not appear in Mayer's version. Among the eighty-eight prayers included here are nearly sixty new translations plus the author's preface and her afterword, thus representing the first time that the majority of Fanny Neuda's original prayer book has appeared in English.

In all previous editions of this book, both in German and in English, the prayers appeared in prose form. For the sake of authenticity, I initially followed suit. However, when I showed the first drafts of my efforts to Ronnie Serr, he suggested that I set them into verse. At first I resisted, wanting to remain as true as possible to Fanny's intention. "Just try it," he said. I did, and the transformation was dramatic. Almost as soon as I introduced line breaks, an inner light seemed to infuse the text, allowing me to see the power of the prayers as never before. I began to hear the underlying music—the rhythms, repetitions, and resonances in the language—and to understand the meaning of the work in a whole new way. This was so exciting to me that I instantly began to ask myself: Why did I study poetry if not for this? Why did I become a book editor if not for this? Why have I been drawn into Jewish study if not for this? Suddenly almost everything I had done in my life, as disconnected as those pursuits may have seemed before, now made perfect sense in the context of this little book of prayers. Even the periods of suffering in my life took on a deeper meaning. I would probably never have been motivated to buy the book in the first place if my son had not been estranged from me, and I might never have sought spiritual sustenance at all if my heart had not been broken. Now, by bringing Fanny's book of prayers back into the world, perhaps I could help guide others, as I had been guided, from suffering to gratitude.

PERSONAL PSALMS

It should come as no surprise that the relationship of poetry and prayer is as old as Hebrew scripture itself. The Torah, or Five Books of Moses, is often referred to as a *shira*, literally "song" or "poem," and the last of the Torah's 613 commandments requires that every Jew write and study the Torah as a *shira*: "Therefore, write down this poem and teach it to the people of Israel; put it in their mouths, so this poem may be my witness against the people of Israel" (Deut. 31:19).

As I began editing Fanny's prayers and setting them in verse, I had the distinct sense that I was releasing the internal poetry contained within them, as if poetry were part of their literary DNA. In fact, some accounts suggest that the emergence of *tkhines*, with their emotional supplications, was stimulated by an early tradition of poetic expression called *piyyut*—from *payyetan*, Greek for "poet"—lyrical prayers that were characterized by expressions of deep religious feeling and love for God.[42]

One of the most illuminating aspects of this work was reinstating the short verses that introduced most of the prayers.[43] These epigraphs, mostly from the Five Books of Moses, the Book of Psalms, Prophets, and other parts of the Hebrew Bible not only attest to the author's knowledge, they also speak to her spiritual depth as a writer. According to Talmudic expression, to write from biblical verse is "to hang by the branches of a tree."

Most of the prayers in this book follow a traditional pattern fundamental to the Book of Psalms, which Fanny must have heard from childhood and studied most of her life. The Psalms of David are considered, next to the Five Books of Moses, to have been most essential to "the development of the Jewish mind and spirit."[44] As her work reveals, Fanny was profoundly influenced by the spiritual power as well as the poetic beauty and depth of these sacred songs to the divine. In her prayer "For Patience and Strength in Adversity," she refers to David as "man of my heart, the holy singer who was captivated by God."

Following a direction that flows through the Psalms, Fanny's prayers tend to move from the heavens above to the earth below, from the universal to the personal. Within each one can also be found the three essential aspects of traditional Jewish prayer: praise/acknowledgment, personal supplication, and thanksgiving. Much like the structure found in biblical psalms, Fanny's prayers are often built in strings of couplets. They also contain internal quotations from Psalms throughout. These elements are all very much in keeping with the earliest compilations of *tkhines*, which were originally written as supplemental prayers to the siddur and reflect its sequence of prayers, many of which also draw from Psalms.[45] Therefore, in both a specific and a general sense, Fanny Neuda's work takes its place within a personal psalm-writing tradition that refers back to the origins of Jewish scripture and extends to the present day.

In "collaborating" with Fanny Neuda in the completion

of this book, I have sought to strike a balance between the sensibility of the author's nineteenth-century voice and accessibility to today's readers. In editing the literal translations,[46] I have aimed for the language and syntax of ordinary speech without distorting meaning. I have trimmed a few of the prayers for length, edited the titles, and reorganized the sequence and grouping of prayers. As for religious and philosophical ideas, I have elected to soften the emphasis on temptation and sin, except where that emphasis was critical to the prayer's intention, and I hope I've been successful in resisting the temptation to interject my own points of view in the editing process.

I considered each opportunity to edit one of Fanny's prayers to be a blessing, and I repeatedly experienced great joy and surprise during the course of this work. One of the most exciting discoveries occurred as I was completing my preliminary edit of the translated material and found, within a long multipart prayer for illness, a "hidden" prayer for a person in the final days of life. The text was so beautiful and deep, I thought it deserved its own place in the book, so I made it into a separate prayer and titled it "At the End of Life."

Throughout the course of this work, I have continued to grow in my respect for Fanny Neuda's gifts both as a writer and as a spiritual teacher. Her personal devotions, each one imbued with deep humility and sincerity, an unwavering reverence for God, generosity toward the less fortunate, and compassion for human suffering, have the power to open the heart and lend courage to all readers—men as well as women, non-Jews and Jews alike. I will always be grateful to have discovered this book and to have been able to serve as a conduit for its rebirth so it might, with God's grace, help others as it has helped me.

May this book of prayers, which has survived for so long and through so much upheaval, continue to endure to bring comfort, healing, and renewal of spirit to all who use it.

May it inspire each of us to find our own words for calling out to God. And finally, may this book be a fulfillment of Fanny's supplication at the end of her prayer "On Purim," that her work might be an ongoing gift to others:

> O God, also grant that whatever powers
> You have given me
> May help me to perform good and useful deeds,
> That my life may not pass away
> Without having borne fruit,
> And that my name may be worthy
> To be praised and blessed
> By those who live with me
> And by those who shall live after me. Amen.

DINAH BERLAND
Los Angeles
23 Adar 5767 (March 13, 2007)

PREFACE TO THE ORIGINAL EDITION

These prayers were not originally written for publication. During my lifetime, so richly filled with the most diverse events, I frequently felt powerful, inescapable urges to enter into dialogue with the sublime Spirit of the Universe— who is enthroned so high and yet sees down so low—that I might find the insight and the strength in God not to stray from or sidestep the path of duty, which so often demanded great sacrifice. That is how most of these prayers were written. In them I found the staff of Moses calling forth to me from the arid rocks of a sad fate, a wellspring of elevating emotions and heavenly consolations—Jacob's ladder, on which the angels of patience, hope, and devotion to God descended from heaven.

For some time many competent parties have encouraged me to present these prayers to the public, but I always resisted subjecting the emotions and thoughts that moved my heart in my loneliest and holiest hours to the judgment of critics. Now, however, my own heart urges me to do so, out of special considerations. Namely, I would like to employ all my meager powers, by publishing these pages, to erect a living memorial to the spirit of my notable late husband, Abraham Neuda, rabbi of Loštice, Moravia, who was taken from me February 22, 1854, at the age of forty-two, after a grave bout of illness in the middle of a life rich in noble and pious deeds. Most of these poems are the outpourings of my heart associated with events I experienced at his side, with him and through him. May his transfigured soul in the life beyond recognize in them the faithfulness and love with which I strove to make his life happy here below.

We already possess some excellent writings in this genre—devotional books for women, penned by men—and mine are scarcely able to stand up to the same scrutiny as those. Nevertheless, the touchstone for the value of such works is without doubt the feelings they evoke and instill in the soul of the person who uses them in prayer. I know that my writings are far from perfect, but nevertheless I hope that, as the product of a female heart, they might echo in women's hearts all the more. A man, however learned and great he may be, cannot capture the essential quality of a woman's experience, cannot as easily reach into the most secret, manifold fibers of the feminine spirit, heed the notes of the most delicate strings, and then give them expression in the living word. A woman, however, need only gaze into her own heart to read the hearts of her sisters, need only call to mind her own experiences to feel their sufferings and joys.

May you, gentle reader, take up this book with goodwill and indulgence, and may God, the All-Knowing, bless it with the power to awaken feelings of devotion in the hearts of those who pray, to grant them solace when they need solace, and to raise them up and sustain them in all periods and events of their lives.

FANNY NEUDA (NÉE SCHMIEDL)
Loštice, Moravia
21 Elul 5614 (September 14, 1854)

1

DAILY PRAYERS

ON ENTERING THE SYNAGOGUE

The name of ADONAI *is a tower of strength*
To which the righteous person runs
And is strengthened.

—PROVERBS 18:10

I greet you, O holy, silent dwelling place,
Splendid temple of God.
Blessed is this hallowed space!
Here is where the Holy One dwells and reigns.
Here I behold the glory of the Almighty,
Whose majesty hovers around me,
And I am embraced by the holiness of God.

Worn down by the cares of life,
I cross the threshold of this sanctuary, and look!
The spirit of peace takes hold of my heart.
Sorrow vanishes, and my soul's anxiety

Gives way to deep and tearful prayer.
Truly, this is the house of God,
And here is the gate that leads to heaven.

Merciful God, you are close to me everywhere,
But closest to me in this place.
Here I feel safe and secure in your protecting hand,
O Protector of All.
Here I feel shielded from life's uncertainties.
Here my soul willingly offers up its sacrifices,
And I gladly place my life at your disposal.
Here I disclose to you my innermost secrets and desires.

Outside in the bustle and turmoil of the world,
Life with its burdens and obstacles rises like a wall
Between my heart and you, O God.
But as I enter these silent, still, and sacred halls
That wall disappears, and my soul rises toward you
Full of joy and enthusiasm, inspiring awe and devotion.
I feel transformed,
For virtue and faith shine brightly here
In their sublime and heavenly forms,
In their eternal, constant majesty.
My very thoughts and emotions are sanctified.
My soul becomes radiant, and my heart opens wide,
Making room for good, noble, and virtuous resolves.

Oh, may this clarity of feeling, this lucid
Contemplation of you, my God and Creator,
Never grow dim,
And may the devotion and holiness
That permeate my heart in this place
Follow me into the outside world.
May this hour become an hour of bliss and grace,
An hour of acceptance,
And may it be pleasing in your eyes,
O merciful and gracious Parent. Amen.

AT MORNING I

Hear my voice, O ADONAI, at daybreak;
At daybreak I plead before you, and wait.

—PSALM 5:4

Almighty God, you bring morning light
Into the place of darkest night.
All creation delights in dawn's brilliance
And exults in the rediscovery of life.
All nature becomes a holy sanctuary, resounding
With the joyous hymns and exultant hallelujahs
It offers up to you, awesome Creator of Worlds.
In the depths, rivers burble their song to you.
From the mountains, mists rise toward you
Like incense from colossal altars.
And so I—but one small being in this vast universe—
Fold my hands in gratitude to you,
And my fervent prayer rises like a child's offering
To your exalted throne.

Last night as I lay bound in slumber, surrounded
By the darkness of night, you watched over me;
Your parental hand hovered over my head,
Shielding me from every danger and fear,
Allowing me to rest in sleep's sweet peace;
And now that I am restored and refreshed
You have once again released my eye
From slumber's shade
So it can freely perceive the beauty of nature
And awaken me to renewed energy and purpose,
To a new delight in life, and to love.

May I spend this day in useful activity.
May I fulfill all my obligations, duties, and tasks
Without pretension but with eagerness,
Neglecting nothing, allotting everything its proper place.
Yet, my God, how the human will wavers,
And how fruitless is any deed or enterprise
That lacks your blessing.
Therefore, I beg of you, All-Gracious God,
May everything I begin with humility and trust in you
Succeed—so my efforts may increase the prosperity
And honor of my home.
May my deeds and spirit be wholesome,
May my work be useful and bring benefit to others,
And may commerce and material profit
Never preoccupy my mind.

Grant me your divine blessings
Of good health, good cheer, and a contented heart
So I might complete my work today
In good spirits and with all my strength.
May I live this day with honesty and integrity,
Never forgetting that the purpose of every day
Is to elevate the soul, make each of us more whole,
And prepare us for the great day
When you transport us to a higher realm.

Benevolent One, let peace and harmony
Reign within my home. Lighten my spirit
So I might earn the love and regard
Of my family and friends.
When some unkindness comes my way,
Help me bear it with composure and patience.
Let only soft silence meet bitter words.
Guard me in times of joy and satisfaction
So I might never give way to arrogance.
In hours of pain, teach me, O God,
To accept your will with humility
And to recognize your presence in everything.
Bless this day for me, that it be a day of goodness,
A day of purpose, a day of success,
A day that sanctifies my life. Amen.

AT MORNING II

ADONAI's mercies are renewed each morning—
Ample is your grace!

—LAMENTATIONS 3:23

My Creator and Sustainer—
Once more the day dawns
And morning's gladdening light
Breaks across the land.
Revived after a refreshing sleep,
I stand before you, O Compassionate One,
Not knowing how to express my gratitude,
Not knowing how to speak to you.

This world, so teeming with wonders,
Is the work of your endless benevolence and love.
You called the earth into being
And made it a home for humanity.

You called forth all the treasures and powers of nature
For our use—you built a human being
From dust and clay
So we might know how fleeting and insignificant
Our earthly work is
And hurry to fulfill our higher purpose—
That we not delay the good we could do in this world
And not reach our final hour
Before completing our true work.
You breathed life into the human body
And granted each of us a spark of your holy spirit
So through it we might recognize your power
And be inspired to strive after you,
To embody your goodness, tenderness, and patience,
And long to be in your presence always.

Ah, but how often we forget the heights, the wisdom,
And the holy purpose to which you have called us.
In our frivolity we forget the Creator's creation,
The Giver's gifts.
We become intoxicated with material pleasures
And forsake heaven for earth.
Caught up in worldly concerns,
We choose the "good life" over doing good deeds,
We choose fleeting pleasures over worthy activity.
We close our conscience to the appeals
Of human justice, lock our hearts against
Our neighbor's cry and our brother's call.
O God and Sovereign, please
Protect me from this way of being.
Let my heart never cling so tightly
To material possessions
That I forget and forsake the higher calling of existence.
May you strengthen my spirit
With the light of your wisdom,
Allowing me to fulfill all my duties with a joyous heart.

May I abandon none of these
And leave none of them aside.
May you fill my heart with warmth and compassion
For those closest to me, so I might ease their troubles
And bring them comfort to the best of my ability.

Please, dear God, allow me and my loved ones
To enjoy your abundant generosity, to discover
All that nourishes and strengthens the body,
All that lifts and elevates the soul,
All that quickens and refreshes the heart.
May you allow us to earn the bread we eat
And the clothes we wear by honorable means,
Free of anxiety or hardship,
Blessed with steady and enduring health.
May we never have to rely on the mercy of others
But rather on your gracious parental hand,
Which is always open, nourishing everything that lives
In mercy and compassion. Amen.

AT EVENING I

By the light of day ADONAI *will command faithful care,*
And even by night the song of the Unseen One is with me,
A prayer to the God of my life.

Parent of All, again a day has passed
And night spreads her somber mantle
Over the earth. Nature rests,
And your human children,
Following her example,
Sink into the embrace of refreshing sleep.
Yet before I close my eyes in slumber
I will raise them in gratitude to you, my Creator.
Before delivering my thoughts and feelings
To the power of sleep,
Let my heart and life engage in communion with you.

My soul delights to think of you, Eternal Parent,
Who, like a human parent, cares for us
In the fullness of love and mercy.
How sweet is it to give thanks to you
And to praise your holy name.
Many are the benefits I received today,
Many the gifts and blessings you bestowed on me.
You caused heaven's light to shine on me
And earth's splendor to captivate my eye.
Your kindness gladdened me,
Your heavenly grace wrapped me in wings of love,
Your merciful hand sustained me and carried me
Through the many threats and dangers
That surrounded me.
All my joy and cheer came from you,
And in my darkest moments
You took my weary head to your parental heart
And strengthened me with heavenly comfort.

Therefore my soul thanks you, my lips praise you,
My heart trusts you in love and confidence,
O Unfathomable One who always gives
And never receives—
You who dispense blessings
And need no blessings for yourself,
You who are an inexhaustible spring
And the font of all goodness and mercy—
Truly you are boundless courage and love.
Yet with fear and trembling I ask myself,
Have I by my works and actions today
Shown myself to be worthy of your love?
Did I spend this day as I should have spent it?
Did I faithfully fulfill all my promises and obligations
To you and to those around me?
When opportunities for goodness came my way,
Did I accept them fully or only in a lukewarm manner

With a cool, unfriendly heart?
Did I honor you in all ways, put my hope in you
And rest my confidence in you?

With grief and remorse I must confess,
I have sinned before you.
I have not always carried you in my heart,
I have not always walked on the path
You prepared for me in your grace and mercy.
My thoughts have not always been caring or generous,
And my actions have not always been patient or calm.
How my conscience stings!
And how easily a painful conscience can rob us
Of our choicest treasure: a peaceful, contented soul.

Be merciful to me, O God of Mercy—
You who are abundant in love and compassion.
Forgive me and do not withdraw
Your grace and love from me now.
Relieve the anxiety of my soul,
And let peace and tranquility descend into my being
So I might enjoy the blessings of sleep
With a contented heart, reconciled with you
And with my conscience.

O Merciful One, let your love watch over me
And guard me from the terrors and dangers
That lurk in the dark.
O God, let the sleep you have granted
For the comfort of all who struggle
Ease all pain and worry.
Let sleep also pour its miraculous balm
Over me and those dear to my heart.
Hide us under the shadow of your wings,
Thus we shall be secure;
For you, O God, are my banner and my sure refuge.

My fortress, my rock, my shield,
Into your hand I entrust my body and my spirit,
My peace and my happiness,
All that is close and precious to me in this life.
Whether I am asleep or awake, God is with me,
And I shall not fear. Amen.

AT EVENING II

Evening shadows recline on the earth.
How refreshing their coolness feels
After the sunlight's brilliant warmth.
How good the calm stillness of evening
After the productivity and bustle of the day,
How good the peaceful sunset
After the day's dazzling shine.
The night sky clouds itself with shining stars,
That appear like God's peace messengers,
Gazing down on us in silence and tranquility,
As if to draw our gaze upward toward the heavens.
Earnest solemnity fills our souls.
A deep, holy feeling flows through us
And lifts our hearts to you, O Unseeable,
Inconceivable One—
You who are ever present, always surrounding us,
Both in night's deepest darkness and in the sun's glare.

I lift up my hands to you, O God,
And thank you from the depths of my soul

For all the blessings of your parental presence,
For every joy that enriches my life, and even
For the sorrow and distress you have laid in my path.
For this too, I will praise you,
Since everything you do is for goodness.
You created this day with everything in it.
Now you bring the night with its strengthening rest.
You watch over sleep, you who neither sleep nor slumber.
Your all-seeing eye rests on those who lie unaware.
You stretch out your shielding hand
Over the sleepers' resting places.
This thought helps me so much.
It lets me know that you are near,
That you are shielding, protecting, and safeguarding me.
Go to your rest, my soul, without trembling or quaking,
For God is with you. What then can you fear?
Strengthen yourselves, my exhausted limbs;
Uplift yourself, my exhausted spirit;
Throw aside your worries and troubles,
Your burdens and weights, my heart,
And surrender yourself to sweet repose.

Yet sleep is gentle and restorative only
With a clear conscience.
Therefore, my protector, before I lay my body down,
I beg you with humility and longing
To forgive and pardon me
If I have been lacking before you today.
If I fell short in my deeds and obligations,
Look forgivingly at my remorse.
Do not withdraw your protection from me,
And let me enjoy an undisturbed and untroubled rest.
May it be your will that I awake in the morning
Refreshed and renewed to useful activity,
To good deeds and good work. Amen.

AT BEDTIME

I lay down—and I slept—
And I awoke again,
Because ADONAI sustains me.

—PSALM 3:6

Sleep—you peaceful, tender angel
Whom God has sent down to this valley of tears
To dampen life's suffering beneath your soft wings—
Descend on my eyelids and bring me rest.
Enter the tents of misery
And cause sweet dreams
To frolic around the beds of the forlorn,
So they might forget their sorrows
And become oblivious to their pain.
Bring healing to the sick that they may awake
Refreshed and strengthened
And feel a renewed, youthful vigor flowing

Through their weary limbs;
And show all who weep over a lost loved one
That death is also but a peaceful sleep
To be followed by a glorious awakening,
A blissful rising into the realms of light,
Where there is no more night or terror of darkness
But heavenly, indescribable bliss
In the presence of God.

Beautiful and profound is the parable
That at night the soul leaves the weary body,
Its shell of dust,
To inscribe the day's deeds
Into the great book of heaven
And that when on some future day
God shall summon each of us
Before the seat of judgment,
The soul's own writing will serve as a testament
To the life each person has lived.
O my soul, may you have only noble thoughts
And worthy deeds to record
In that book of everlasting memorial. Amen.

ON SUNDAY

God said, "Let there be light."

Sovereign and Creator of the World,
A new week has begun.
This first day of the week evokes the spirit
Of the great first day of creation,
When all was in chaos and bleak,
When endless darkness rested over the awesome abyss.
All at once you spoke—
And out of the terrifying lap of darkness,
A joyful, brilliant light emerged,
The first cause and condition of all life and being.

Day after day your almighty "becoming"
Resounded anew through the chambers of creation.
Each day the circle of your creations expanded further.
New energies, new forms

Passed before the Light of Existence
Until they emerged into the world
As manifest beings, imprinted
With your exalted glory and majesty, reflections
Of your all-encompassing wisdom and goodness.
Then the day of heavenly rest
Sealed the week so rich with creation,
And you blessed it and hallowed it
For rest and celebration for all time.

My God, it would not have been too difficult
Nor too much for you
To accomplish the entire work of creation
In a single day, through a single, solitary word,
Through a single, solitary breath.
Yet you wanted to impart to us the great teaching
That every day of the week was ordained
For work and for labor, that a person
Shall let no day pass in useless activity or idleness;
For the day that we do not make noteworthy
Through useful action and work
Is a day forever lost to us,
Stricken from the book of our lives.

Grant, O God, that I might live
True to this conviction, that I might
Fill my days with wise activity.
May you, God of strength, stand by me.
May you, source of all wisdom, enlighten me
Through your understanding and insight,
So in everything I undertake, I keep
A good and worthy goal before my eyes
And always find the right means to accomplish it.

O God, lend strength and good health to my body.
Lend patience and endurance to my spirit

So I can manage all the tasks and expectations
Of my position and my calling,
That I never tire or become weary
As I approach the place where duty and conscience lead.
Let my spirit shine with the light of awareness
And faith. Let it never be cloaked and shadowed
By corruption's dull shroud, nor let the false lights
Of material possessions lead me astray.

At last, when I come to the end of my life's week,
When I stand at the threshold that leads to eternal rest
And gaze back at my fulfilled labor and work,
Let the joyful awareness that "it was good"
Be worthy of my mortal conviction
And of your divine grace. Amen.

ON MONDAY

God said, "Let there be an expanse
In the midst of the water
And let it separate water from water." . . .
God called the expanse "Sky."

—GENESIS 1:6–8

I look up, my God and Sovereign,
To the beautiful sky, so full of wonders,
That you have cast above the earth.
I gaze up at the vast expanse of blue—
At the clouded heights from which you speak
In the solemn, commanding language
Of thunder and lightning.
I look up and my gaze rests with awe on these heavens
That you have clothed so gloriously in wonder.
Oh, how poor we would have been
If you hadn't, in your grace, granted us this view!
What would the earth have been for us—

How sad, how barren, how joyless,
If you hadn't given us the sky?
We cast our dearest hopes into the heavens;
Our spirits yearn toward its heights.
Our gaze turns toward it in times of joy and sorrow,
On good days and on bad. From the heavens
We draw joy and strength into our hearts.
Yes, O Holy One, your throne lies
At the pinnacle of heaven. Your seat rests
In the distant heights beyond all heights;
Yet, for all that, you are never far
From your earthly children.
Your justice and your compassion
Reign over the whole world,
Yet you carry the smallest of your creations
Close to your heart. You guide them
With a faithful parental hand.

Preserve for me, Parent of All, an eye forever open
To the wondrous works of your creation.
Preserve in me a consciousness forever open to you,
All-Wise, Almighty, All-Loving Creator
And Parent of All.
Preserve in me an open heart
In which to instill an all-encompassing love—
A love for you, O God, and for all your creations.
May strength and courage always dwell in my heart
Along with the intention and energy
To practice goodness and to pursue
All that is life-giving and blessed
For me, for my loved ones, and for all my neighbors.
Preserve for me the heaven of this life,
Pure and untroubled by grief and suffering.
Enlighten it through the blessed light
Of your grace and mercy, which you never withhold,
And draw me into it—me and all my loved ones
And the great, vast world of humanity. Amen.

ON TUESDAY

And God said, "Let the earth sprout vegetation:
Seed-bearing plants, fruit trees of every kind
That bear fruit with seed in it."

—GENESIS 1:11

A profound emotion stirs within me
Whenever I witness the richness
Of your blessèd creation. How much beauty,
How many wondrous forms and forces
We encounter in which all your glory and faithfulness,
Your boundless parental love,
Are made manifest and visible!
What could the limited mortal heart wish for itself
That your magnificent, bountiful creation
Has not already provided in abundance?
All that strengthens and nurtures the body,
All that quickens and buoys the heart,

All that ennobles and elevates the spirit—
You have spoken all this into being for us.
You let your holy word spread over the earth,
And the ground sprouted countless seeds and seedlings,
Oceans of grain and fruit-bearing trees,
Flowers of myriad colors and healing herbs.
You sent forth bubbling springs, blustering storms,
Seas too vast for human vision.

When my heart reflects on all of this,
Hope and trust flow into my being.
The One who created and established
This world so full of wonders
As a home for all humanity—
The One who arranged it
To satisfy our hungers and please the eye
As well as to revive and enliven the spirit—
Doesn't this Holy One, so full of love,
Also gaze down on human beings
With a heart overflowing with parental love?
Won't this God allow the trees
Of well-being and good fortune to blossom for us
And let the flowers of joy sprout forth?
Won't this God command his angels
To carry us in their arms?
The God who set limits for the sea,
Keeping the dry land from being deluged by it,
That God also commands the tears that express my pain
And dries them from my cheeks,
Replacing them with the blush of joy.

Sustainer of seeds and new shoots,
You who called them into being
On the third day of creation,
May you also preserve in me
The seeds and new shoots of these hopeful thoughts:

That storms and scorching sun not harm them
But instead that they embed themselves within my heart
And come to bear lush, abundant fruit;
That the world might take joy from them
And that you, my God, might find them pleasing.
Amen.

ON WEDNESDAY

God said, "Let there be lights in the firmament
To separate day from night."

—GENESIS 1:14

You who reign amid eternal light—
My tongue praises you.
My heart rises up to you in humility and trust.
My eye does not glimpse you.
My understanding does not encompass you.
Yet my heart knows you and my soul recognizes you
In the shining mirrors of your wonder
That reveal your presence anew each day.
On the fourth day of creation
Your magnificent power was made manifest
In the brilliant lights of the firmament—
Flaming orbs that cross the highest heights,
According to your word and will.

You spoke: "Let there be light"—
And sent light beaming through
The vast reaches of creation.
The sun burst forth in the heavens
And suffused everything
With overflowing brilliance and energy.

Then the moon was drawn up into the evening sky,
Silent and tranquil—the companion of lovers,
From whose dwellings slumber flees;
Comforter of the sorrowful,
Who trust their pain to the night's quiet.
The moon gleams amid an infinity of stars—
A multitude of cheerful, sparkling eyes
That gaze down on us
Like guardians of our destinies,
Uplifting our souls.

O God, how great and full of endless love
And mercy you are, that you have spread
So much light and splendor across creation.
Your light fills my heart
With adoration and nobility of spirit.
It bolsters my courage and trust on the grayest days.
You have set the heavenly lights in their courses
And established the proper times
For their rising and setting.
At day's end you bring night's stillness
To give rest and slumber to your weary earth,
And after the night, you allow
A new dawn to break to refresh and renew
Everything that has slumbered and slept.
So, too, will you send us your comforting, heavenly light
When nights of adversity and misfortune
Darken our souls.
When worries and troubles cloud our lives,

You will let the sun of your holy grace and mercy
Shine above us once more.
When devastating fortunes threaten to devour us,
You will unfurl evening's shadow.
And so will I begin my day's work, Eternal Parent,
With this confidence and trust in you:
That you will bless us from the fullness of your grace,
Shining the light of abundant well-being
On me and my loved ones. Amen.

ON THURSDAY

How abundant are your works, O ADONAI!
With wisdom you made them all.

—PSALM 104:24

How great are your works, O God!
One day proclaims your wonders to the other.
One day tells the other
Of your grace and love for all your creatures.

On the fifth day of the week
Your creative will called forth all life on earth.
How manifold and countless are your creations
That inhabit this earthly sphere.
They exist in so many different forms, qualities,
Natures, and ways,
Yet your parental eye watches over them all.
Your parental concern hovers over each kind—

Over those that live in the dry, barren wilderness,
Over those that live in rich, green valleys,
Over those that soar through the air,
Over those that dwell in the depths of the sea—
You watch over them and are mindful of them all.
They call to you in the language of their need,
And you hear them.
You fulfill the need of each one.
How then can you not rest your gaze on me,
To whom you have given so much
And before whom you have displayed
Such bountiful signs of your grace and love?

Therefore I praise you, my God,
With joy and good cheer.
With a glad heart I will fulfill the duties required
By my calling and my place in this great chain of being.
I will not give in to despair over my wants and needs.
You who give life also provide the means
To sustain us and make life possible.
You who provide grain for the animals in the field
And to the young ravens who cry out for food—
You will not exclude me from your gifts of charity.

I pray to you for one thing alone, Eternal Parent:
Lend me insight and understanding
That I might enjoy your gifts
With a wise and perceptive heart
And never misuse your blessings.
Enlighten me, whom you have elevated
Above the animals of the field,
That I might appreciate and act from my higher self,
Not dwell at the basest level of my nature
But instead always strive to become a better person,
Ever more worthy of your generous gifts,
And continue to raise myself ever higher

Toward you, who created human beings
For a holy life on earth
And toward a blessed home in the world to come.
Amen.

ON FRIDAY

God said, "Let us make a human being
In our image and likeness."

You are great, O God,
In your visible wonders and works
But greater still in your invisible laws and blessings.
In the six days of creation your almighty word
Called this great and beautiful earth into existence,
The world and everything that fills it—
Animals and plants, refreshing dew and lustrous sun.
And when the world was finished in all its glory,
You placed human beings into it so we might know
All your glorious works, enjoy all created things,
And praise you who are so good and gracious.

All-Merciful One, worlds praise you,
Choirs of angels sing everlasting hymns to you.

Therefore, why shouldn't humans, children of earth,
Also worship and praise you, since you have
Singled us out, have especially remembered
And blessed us in your embracing love,
Have honored and exalted us?
Indeed, O God, I will adore you and praise you
With a life of virtue, full of reverence for you
And love for my neighbor,
And I will always be grateful for your goodness.
You formed and created me in your own image.
You gave me a body, beautiful and noble
In shape and form. You gave me
A spirit even nobler and more exalted,
A ray from your wisdom, the light of your love,
And have united both
Into one glorious, wonderful whole.
Should I then deface this masterpiece of creation
By mistreatment? Should I abuse my body,
Deprive it of its beauty with bad habits and excesses
Or by malice, hatred, envy, or jealousy?
Should I deprive my spirit of its nobility
By unworthy sentiments or aspirations,
By unhealthy practices?
No! I will carefully attend to myself,
Ennoble my heart by acts of charity,
Elevate my spirit by your teachings and your divine law.
I will guard my body, this frail garb of the soul,
Against every damaging influence, against anything
That may endanger its health or weaken its energies;
For the body is the creation of your hands,
The means and instrument of our labors on this earth.

May you, O God, help me strengthen my resolve.
May you guard me against despair,
So that want and suffering, grief and sorrow
May never overpower me,

So bodily affliction and pain
May not dim my soul's light,
So mental grief and suffering
May not weaken and destroy my body too soon,
So I might always aspire heavenward
To offer you my body's vigor and my heart's glow
Until you, in your inscrutable judgment,
Shall separate my soul from my body,
Allowing my spirit to wing its way up to you,
To dwell again with you, O Source of Being,
Who is and shall remain
From eternity to eternity. Amen.

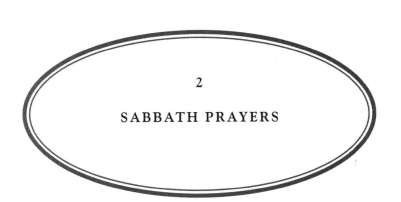

2

SABBATH PRAYERS

FOR BAKING CHALLAH
חַלָּה

God in heaven, according to
Your holy commandment, I set aside
A portion of my bread dough for you.
This pious custom reminds me
Not only of our people's past—
Of how our ancestors laid their first fruits
At your altar with joyous hearts—
But also that even today
We can bring God-pleasing offerings
To the altar of love and humanity:
When we relieve the hunger of the poor,
Satisfy their needs, soften their misery,
And ease their worries,
We are making these offerings to you,
Parent of the poor and unfortunate.

So, Parent of All, accept this challah offering.
Make my heart firm and faithful
That I may also be prepared to bring

Greater and higher offerings before you
With faithful joy and willingness.

Bless this, our daily bread, O Holy One,
That we may earn it in honor and without suffering
That its enjoyment may bring us blessing and prosperity,
That we may savor life and all its goodness
In the fullness of health and strength,
That we may bring cheerful and elevating spirits
To our praise of you, Giver of All Goodness,
And fully dedicate ourselves to all our duties.
Praised are you, ADONAI, *our God,*
Sovereign of the Universe,
Who has made us holy through your commandments
And has commanded us to separate challah. Amen.

AS SABBATH ENTERS—
AFTER CANDLE LIGHTING

Praised are you, ADONAI, *our God,*
Sovereign of the Universe,
Who has made us holy through your commandments
And has commanded us to kindle the Sabbath lights.

—TRADITIONAL BLESSING

Almighty God, with joyful emotions I light,
At your command and behest, these candles
As ornaments and as glorification of the Sabbath hours,
Which you have hallowed and made holy.
How sweet, how precious are these hours
That, by your grace, you have given us.
Oh, how the calm Sabbath stillness
Rejoices our hearts, offering rest to the body
For the toils and labors of the week,
While the spirit soars up to you

On wings of holy meditation
And the heart seeks and finds you
With fervent prayer, with pious attention
To the proclamation of your holy word
And in undisturbed contemplation
Of your boundless love.
Many are the cares and sorrows of the weekdays,
Many the struggles in life, but when Sabbath appears,
Rest and peace enter our hearts.
Restless desires, exciting aspirations,
And struggles for earthly gifts and treasures give way
To sweet mental repose, and the heart opens
To receive calm, pleasant, and quieting emotions.

O Compassionate One, how can we thank you enough
For all your grace and goodness?
Throughout the week you surrounded us
With your protection and mercy.
Your kind parental grace blessed us
With life and health, with nourishment and clothing,
With light and warmth.
You prepared a thousand pleasures for us
That rejoiced our hearts,
Often even before we were aware of them.
From day to day the manna of your heavenly blessings
Has come down for us, and at the end of a week
So full of your manifold gifts you have granted us
The choicest of all heavenly blessings: the Sabbath day.
Shabbat is the crown and glorious ornament of the week.
It ennobles our aspirations, consecrates our enjoyment,
Pours soft, heavenly light
Across our pilgrim path on earth,
And carries us back to you
Whenever weekday aspirations remove us from you.
We look up to you, O God,
With pure confidence, in love and humility.

Every thought of you lifts the veil from our eyes,
The light increases within our souls,
And we feel the certainty of a better future,
A higher Sabbath in your presence—
Where the weary pilgrim, in the lustrous light
Beaming from your throne, enters into everlasting rest,
Where the gates of Eden open
For the pious and righteous who have accomplished
Their span of years and fulfilled their destination.
The harder our labors shall have been on earth,
The sweeter will be their fruits;
The more industrious the laborer,
The richer the laborer's reward.

Bless then, O my God, these holy hours,
That they may bring me
Their elevating and quickening power,
That they may afford renewal and strength to my body,
Understanding and enlightenment to my spirit,
That I may ever improve in my knowledge of you
And so learn to walk in your ways,
Becoming ever more worthy of your benevolence.
Grant your almighty protection
To me and my loved ones.
Guard us against all accident and evil,
Guide us in our quest for virtue,
And cause the light of joy to burn in our hearts
And the light of love and peace
To shine in our homes. Amen.

ON THE SABBATH DAY
שַׁבָּת

Sabbath's blessing is eternal
When we but understand its call,
Not only to cultivate rest
But to receive its gift of sanctity.

—SALOMON MAIMON
(German, 1754–1800)

My God and Holy Parent,
My Creator and Sustainer,
In six days your divine word called forth
This entire magnificent world out of nothing,
And on the seventh day you established
Your blessing and your sanctification,
Making it a day of rest for all people.
On this day all enterprise takes a holiday,
All creative work is completed,
And the noise of workshops and factories

Grows quiet in the streets.
Our houses are cheerfully adorned,
And our hearts are uplifted.
A festive glow brightens our homes.
This is the Sabbath, to honor the Source of Being.
The purpose and goal of the Sabbath
Is not to descend into a useless idleness
In which the spirit sinks
And we indulge in thoughtless desires;
The purpose and goal of the Sabbath
Is to afford relaxation to our bodies
So our souls might unfurl to their full capacities.
This is the outer being's rest
So the inner being may emerge with greater vitality
And our better selves may reach
Their fullness and power.
On the Sabbath we put aside service to the world
And dedicate ourselves instead
To the service of God.
We lay down our work for our earthly portion
And allow ourselves to live whole, undivided lives
For our spiritual, eternal redemption—
So we are not flooded
By a stream of worldly concerns and struggles,
So our moral convictions
And the highest stirrings of our hearts
Do not get lost amid the demands of our lives,
So the noisy cries of the outside world
Do not overwhelm and silence the holy songs within.

So will I, my God and Sovereign,
Obey your commandments and turn to
Spiritual pursuits on this holy day.
I will elevate my heart through your divine words,
And before all else I will read from your sacred Torah—
Of your wonders and your power,
Of your wisdom, your grace, and your compassion—

So I may always come to recognize your presence
And learn to honor you more humbly,
So I may always follow you with childlike devotion;
So I may always love you with my whole heart,
With my whole soul, and with my whole might.

I will pass the Sabbath hours by attending to
The development of my children's hearts
And by imprinting the lessons
Of virtue and faith within their souls.
I will let the spirit of love, trust in God,
And generosity hold sway in my environment
To the extent of my own strengths and abilities.

Yet I will focus my thoughts not only
On the members of my own household but also
On the wider circle of my friends and neighbors.
I will seek out those poor and suffering souls
Whom I might be able to aid through counsel or deed.
Thus will I celebrate this day,
To remember the Sabbath and keep it holy
In truth as well as in practice.

O God, strengthen my will toward this always.
Grant me wisdom, strength, and endurance
To make your will manifest.
Grant that the feelings and sentiments of the Sabbath
That stir my soul today
Accompany me tomorrow
Through the activities of the week
So that even amid the busy workday
I may carry the sense of Sabbath in my soul,
So my heart may always become purer,
So my spirit may always become more complete,
Until it becomes refined and is brought to perfection
To celebrate its great Sabbath rest
In the world to come. Amen.

IN PRAISE OF THE ONE
(BEFORE עָלֵינוּ)

God, I see you everywhere, wherever I gaze—
From low valleys to lofty mountains,
A sweet song resounds:
"One of God's great hands
Spanned the heavens,
Creating angels and worms,
Summer's breeze and winter's storms."

—SALOMON MAIMON

You, High Exalted One—
In humility and awe, I bow down before you,
To your majesty that extends through all time,
Throughout all worlds.
My heart, burning with thanks and love,
Brings its songs of praise and exaltation to you here.
How great, how majestic you are!
All this came into being at your single nod.

Your hand laid out the earth's foundations.
Your hand spanned over this planet, over this
Brilliant, gleaming, star-speckled ceiling of sky.
Your hand creates, your breath gives life
To everything that breathes and all that stirs.
Your love is the single, solitary force
That lifts and carries, protects and embraces.
You are One and Only in the heavens and on earth.
Your power alone moves in the thundering cloud
And in the ocean's flood.
You guide the scorching windstorm through the desert,
You lead the multitude of stars
In their orderly progression across the sky
And send blessed beams of sunlight down to earth.
You, One and Only, always present and everywhere—
Wherever I am and everywhere I look,
I find you, the One, the Eternal,
The protector and refuge of all.

Therefore, I bend my knee before you alone.
I pray to you from out of the dust.
I lift my eyes to you in times of trouble
And in times of joy. I raise up to you
All the wishes and hopes of my heart.

How unfortunate are those whose hearts
Are too closed to be able to feel you,
Whose spirits are so blind they are unable to see you,
Who do not perceive you in your works,
Who do not recognize the invisible
In the visible realm of nature—in this mirror
That reflects your majesty and greatness.
Oh, open the eyes of those who do not see.
Purify the hearts of those
Who have turned away from you—
Whether from the fatigue of sorrow and suffering

Or from the idolatry of worldly diversions—
That all inhabitants of this earth
May turn back to you,
That all knees may bend before you,
That all hearts may stream toward you,
That all lips may pour out praise and exaltation
To you, that your name—
The One, Eternal, Full of Wonders—
Be celebrated and made known
Through all times and all places. Amen.

AFTER THE PRIESTLY BLESSING

Let them place my name on the people of Israel,
And I shall bless them.

—NUMBERS 6:27

All-Compassionate One, Let your blessing
That we have received at this hour, the blessing
That holy priests once bestowed on your people,
Fulfill us. May it prove true for us
In its entire fullness and meaning, in every part.

Bless us, O God!

For you alone are the source
Of all blessing and well-being.
Bless us with the rich and manifold gifts of existence.
Bless us with firm and lasting health, with long life,
And with the strength to practice goodness

And do what pleases you.
Bless us in all that we begin.
Bless us through our children
And our children's children,
That they may grow to be our joy and honor.

And protect us.

Protect what you have given us
And what you continue to give.
Protect us, All-Compassionate One,
From all accidents and misfortunes.
Protect us from the loss
Of true friends and beloved family.
Protect us from hunger and want.
Protect us from becoming dependent
On flesh and blood.
Protect us in all that we love and honor.

Shine your countenance upon us.

May we feel your presence
In its holy tenderness and warmth,
May it illuminate the earthly night and fog.
Kindle in our souls the light of truth
With which to recognize you, O God,
And to perceive your eternal goodness and majesty.

And be gracious to us.

Your mercy alone is our hope and our rescue.
Be a gracious, mild, and merciful judge for us
In our waywardness and in our transgressions.
Take us to your heart in love and tenderness
When we return to you like regretful children.
Let your grace and mercy rest on us

Wherever and whenever we need it,
Whenever we call on you.

Turn your countenance toward us.

Your gaze rests on us, encouraging us
In all that is good and just,
Restraining us from doing wrong.
Your presence, which is always with us,
Is our comfort and our refuge in suffering,
Even when all turn away—
When father and mother, friends and children,
Forsake us—you never forsake us
But turn your compassion toward us.

And grant us peace.

May we be at peace with the world and with ourselves,
The peace of a tranquil conscience
And fulfilled obligations.
Let hate, envy, jealousy, and misunderstanding—
Everything that stirs up conflict and discord—
Flee from us. Grant us peace, O God,
Your true, pure, flowing peace.
And, at the end, let us go forth from here in peace,
Gazing back on our lives with the satisfaction
Of a fully lived life, to find eternal peace with you,
The joy of heaven in your presence
And blessedness in your law. Amen.

ON THE SABBATH
BEFORE THE NEW MOON
שַׁבָּת רֹאשׁ חֹדֶשׁ

And to the moon, God spoke:
"Let it renew itself
And be a gleaming, wondrous sight
For the children of the earth."

—ANONYMOUS PRAYER

I praise and thank you,
God and Sovereign of the Universe.
With your words, you created the heavens,
And with one breath of your majesty,
You created all of its shining hosts!
You set each one on its course
And to its appointed place
So its position and progress are never confounded.
To the moon, you spoke: *Let it renew itself*

And be a gleaming, wondrous sight
For the children of the earth,
That its thinning and renewing light
Might be a reflection of our own shifting, changing
Lives below. From high above
The moon offers comfort and support,
Admonishment and warning.

To the unfortunate, the moon says:
Poor heart, do not dwell on your suffering.
Do not bemoan the gloom and fogginess of your path
Or how your life has become as dark as night.
Look at me! Your fortune can't be gloomier
Or more difficult than my own waning light was
But a few short days ago—and look now!
Already you can see me shining above you.
So, too, your fortune will shift.
Grief is not permanent.
God is not always angry!
So don't complain, and don't become anxious.
Bear with endurance and courage
The burdens that God has given you.
Soon the Eternal One will let you shine once more
In the brilliance of divine mercy.
Soon the Eternal One will guide you
Out of darkness and into the light.

To the fortunate and honored, the moon warns:
Oh, lucky one, don't be so proud,
Don't act so haughty or great,
Though the glitter and dazzle of fortune surround you
And the road of life lies bright and shining before you.
Look at me and see how I, too,
Bask in my own light now,
But in a short time I will have darkened
And become a dim object;

People will search for me to no avail.
In the same way, human fortunes travel
In their own orbits.
Before you know it, you, too, will fall
Into the dark night and misfortune's misery.
Therefore, be humble and modest.
Let your brilliance enter the shadowed huts of suffering
And brighten the dark misfortune nearest to you.
Offer gentle comfort wherever and whenever you can
To downtrodden and suffering hearts.

To the young, the moon speaks
With muted yet mighty eloquence:
You who stand in the new moon of life,
Take my model as your teacher.
Just as my light increases from day to day
And I climb higher in my path, so may you increase
The light and strength of your spirit each day
And always strive to rise higher
Along the path of your convictions.
Don't fall into a painful night of ignorance,
Letting life pass you by unnoticed
In darkness, in uselessness.
Rather, let your life brighten and gladden the world
With the shining brilliance of wisdom and virtue.

To the elder one, however,
Who enters the last quarter of life dimmed and bent,
With the light ever waning and fading,
The moon speaks comfort from its heights,
As the rising of every new moon
Reminds us of the heavenly promise of life to come:
For God spoke to the moon: *Let it renew itself*
And be a gleaming, wondrous sight
For the children of the earth,
That they, like it, should be renewed and rejuvenated

For the glory and honor of their Creator.
Just as the moon fades and slips away before our eyes,
Only to rise once more in a younger, renewed form,
So it is with the eternal, unblemished nature
Of the human soul.
Here the light of a person's life is waning,
But there, in the other realm, where there is no change
But only eternity and perpetual joy,
The soul's light shines brightly and will never dim.

So, All-Compassionate One, may the moon
Renew itself as a redemption and a blessing
For me and for all humanity.
May its comforting, uplifting face
Always be before our eyes, and may the sight of it
Place hope and security, courage and trust,
And noble intentions and strivings in our hearts.

May the coming month bring me and my loved ones
All we require for our well-being—
Health of soul and body, peace within and without,
The blessed fruits of our labors, and a fertile seed
For our eternal redemption. Amen.

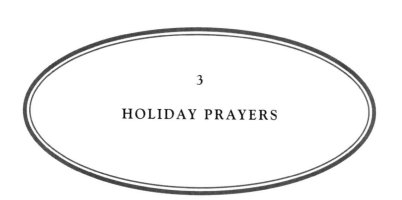

3

HOLIDAY PRAYERS

ON THE NEW MOON
רֹאשׁ חֹדֶשׁ

Teach us to number our days,
Then we shall gain a heart of wisdom.

—PSALM 90:12

God of life, who regulates the course of time,
You have divided it into great and small periods,
Into years, months, and days.
These passages teach us how time rushes by
In swift, uninterrupted flight
And with every onward movement carries us nearer
To the end of all earthly existence—into eternity—
And that fleeting time, once gone,
Will never reverse its course
Despite all our wishes and ardent desires for its return.
Therefore we must use it
As long as we can still call it ours

And waste not even the least bit of it—
Lose no hours by useless deed or practice,
For you, O God, will on some future day,
Call us to account for how we spent our lives.

We must carry out our works and complete them
As time lays them out before us.
If we contemplate them too much and hesitate,
Then the stream of time tugs them past us,
And all that remains are empty hindsight and regret.
Whatever we begin and undertake,
Whatever we struggle with and strive for—
May they be healing and God-pleasing works,
Expressing our highest convictions on earth,
Worthy of beings who were made in the image of God.

Therefore, O Heavenly Protector, I pray to you
For understanding and wisdom that I may use my time
In ways that are a blessing to me, to my loved ones,
And to my fellow human beings—
That I may use every hour, every moment of my life,
In wise action and effort, in valuable work and study,
For the ennoblement of my heart, for the preparation
And cultivation of my soul—for eternity.
O Compassionate One, who has always
Guided and shielded me, continue to grant
Your gracious protection to me and my loved ones.
May the coming month
Be a month of peace and joy for us.
Preserve our health and lives,
Soften and lighten our grief,
Increase our pleasure in life,
Bless the works of our hands,
And grant us, in the fullness of your grace,
All that we may need
And all that may be good for us. Amen.

ON THE FIRST DAYS OF PASSOVER
פֶּסַח

Dear God, the festival of Passover has come—
The joyful feast memorializing the days of jubilee,
When you redeemed our ancestors
From inhuman oppression and carried them
With an outstretched hand
Into the beautiful land of liberty,
From the dark dwellings of error and false belief
Into the sunny realms of knowledge and the pure,
Gladdening faith in you and your divine word.

With deep emotion and joy, we celebrate this holiday,
Which reminds us of that happy time
When you chose Israel for your inheritance,
Elected her from all nations,
Wedded her to you as a bridegroom weds his bride
And bound her to you with the ties of grace and love—
The time when your people, in return, clung to you,
As a youthful bride to the heart of her beloved,
As a child to its mother's breast—

When they followed you, full of love and faithfulness
Into a strange, unknown land,
Followed you into a vast desert wilderness.

A long space of time has since passed,
And the heart of your people has often changed,
But your love has always remained the same.
You have been a help and refuge
To our ancestors from eternity,
A shield and a help to their children after them
Throughout all generations.
You are our guide, our protector, our guardian,
As you have been in all times.

We have passed through more than one Egypt.
Hatred and prejudice have set
A heavy yoke around our necks,
But through the darkness of misery and oppression
A ray of your grace has continually shone above us
And has at last brought a morning of redemption
In which our human dignity is recognized
And we live free and undisturbed
Under the protection of mild and just laws.
Oh, may you, O God, continue to be with us.
As in the days when you burst the chains
In which we sighed, and with an awful hand
Broke the yoke of bondage and tyranny,
So may you deliver and redeem our souls
That they may rise above all attacks
From within or without.
As you hurled the many idols and gods of Egypt
From their altars, so may your boundless mercy
Release us from the idols that attract us today,
And let every cell and organ of our bodies be filled
With your incomparable, exalted, and glorious being.
May we be thoroughly infused by faithfulness and love,

By unconditional, unwavering confidence,
And boundless attachment to you.
You are the shield and savior of every human being
As well as of whole nations.
You comfort them
In the midst of trouble and suffering. Amen.

ON THE LAST DAYS OF PASSOVER

God's strength and cutting power
Were my deliverance.

—EXODUS 15:2

Today we celebrate the day to be remembered always
When our ancestors crossed through the sea.
With jubilation and wonder, our hearts incline
Toward the blessed Sea of Reeds—
A symbol of unparalleled wonder
Through which you made manifest
The freedom and redemption of our ancestors.

The Israelites' need was great.
Before them lay the tumultuous sea.
Behind them were countless legions of Egyptians,
A mighty, well-practiced army against weaponless slaves.
No hope and no road lay open for the downtrodden

To escape the terrible might of their pursuers.
Yet you are the rescuer of the pursued,
The counselor of the oppressed,
The avenger of the innocent;
And you saw their distress.
You heard their cry in time of crisis,
And you opened an awesome path for them,
A path no human foot had ever trod,
A path no human stride had ever trampled.
Your powerful word resounded
Over the torrential waters:
The voice of God over the waters,
The voice of God over the roaring waves.
The floodwaters at the sea's heart were astonished;
Streams of water formed into firm walls,
And the depths became a safe, smooth road
For the people of Israel to cross.
Out of swells and eddies you built them a bridge
On which they were lifted up and carried.
With your might, you ferried them across
To safe harbor,
But under the feet of their pursuers
The seafloor sank once more. The waters descended,
And Pharaoh and his army tumbled into the surge.
The floodwaters raged over them, seething high
Into the foaming, billowing sea.
God's punishment followed the offenders
To the depths of the abyss.

Endless hallelujahs resounded
From the mouths of the saved.
This is my God, and I will praise ADONAI,
For ADONAI *is exalted.*
The child nursing at its mother's breast
Joined its voice to the victory song of Moses and Israel,
The same song we sing in our synagogues today

For your name's honor and glory.
So, too, O my soul, praise the Holy One.
Praise the One who humbles the proud
And raises up the humble and mild.
The Holy One is our guardian and protector
In times of trouble.
God was, God is, and God will be our refuge forever.

The time of visible, manifest wonders
May have long passed. Nature may no longer
Step off its track on our behalf.
Yet your eternal might, my God, still surrounds us.
Your miraculous power still works,
Silently and invisibly, to assist us.
Nature's factories remain in perpetual operation
To produce everything that aids and benefits us.
When we—pursued, oppressed, or lost—seek escape,
You still show us the path of our redemption,
The path of rescue and hope.
Sometimes it is a faithful friend
Who helps and counsels us;
Sometimes it is the inner voice of the heart,
The angel of God within us, who guides us,
Safe and unharmed, across the sea of life,
Over waves where you, O God, reign
And where billowing surf alternately rages and subsides
According to your almighty will.

Therefore rejoice, O my soul, in the Source of Being
And continue onward in faith and humility.
When life's sky turns cloudy
And when the ground beneath your feet
Threatens to give way, don't lose heart.
Don't falter in your trust in God.
The Eternal One will come to your aid at the right time.
For all our help comes from the Eternal One.

Entrust your way to God
And God will smooth the way.
For the Sovereign of All is the might and the power,
The glory and the mercy forever. Amen.

ON THE FESTIVAL
OF RECEIVING THE TORAH
שָׁבוּעוֹת

Remember the Torah of Moses, my servant.

—MALACHAI 3:22

With reverent emotions I greet this festive day,
Israel's initiation feast,
The memorial of that great season
That brought so much hope and blessing to the world.
Amid the roar of thunder and flashes of lightning,
You, O God, descended onto the modest brow of Sinai
And spoke to your people
In your sublime yet tender language.
You, the Infinite One, came down
To your finite human children
To reveal yourself to us in your glory and majesty
And give us statutes of justice and truth,
Doctrines of comfort and redemption.

This joyous festival honors the receiving
Of our highest treasure, our most precious jewel:
The Ten Commandments, the pillar
And cornerstone of our faith,
Our true guide and leader through life,
Pointing out the paths of virtue and duty.
This support and saving anchor
During sorrow and trouble contains everything
That elevates the spirit, ennobles the heart,
Causes adults to be more mature
And children more childlike,
Affords consolation to the despairing
And confidence to those in doubt.

1   *I am ADONAI, your God, who brought you out of the
     land of Egypt, out of the house of bondage.*

These are the first words of divine revelation.
Oh, how blessed are these glorious words to me—
Words that the heart proclaims in a still, small voice
You call out to the world in resounding tones.
With your seal and endorsement, you provide
Words that are inscribed
On every page of the book of nature:
There is a God!—a God of supreme power,
Who crushed our oppressors and persecutors
With a mighty arm; a God of compassion,
Who listens to the lamentations
Of the oppressed and enthralled,
Who breaks all bars and chains
To lead them into freedom and happiness.
Oh, how my heart expands with joy and confidence
In the One who, with infinite love,
Also reaches out to me
Whenever sorrow and oppression surround me,
Whenever the hand of persecution weighs down on me,
Whenever the gates of happiness are closed before me.

2   *You shall have no other gods before me.*

The Eternal One alone is God, and to God alone
Belong all glory, praise, and adoration.
O my heart, dedicate your worship,
Your love, and your thankfulness to God.
It is God alone who graciously leads me through life,
My Creator and Rescuer, who guides my youth,
Guards my old age,
And is always and everywhere the same—
In the heavens above, on the earth below,
In the depths of the sea.
Therefore, be of good cheer and courage, my soul.
Though your destiny may not be fortunate,
Though grief and pain may weigh you down,
Bear it all with patience and acceptance,
Hopefully and trustfully,
For God, the All-Wise and All-Loving,
Our sole Guardian and Sovereign, who in wisdom
Creates storms as well as sunlight,
Has designed it for you, and whatever God does
Can only be for our redemption.
The Holy One will make all things right.

3   *You shall not speak God's name in falsehood.*

How can we utter in untruth
The name of the One whose whole being
Is truth and faithfulness?
Faithfulness and sincerity
Are rays of God's divine being.
They ennoble the heart that receives them
And elevate it to the image of the Eternal.
Oh, may these holy feelings never depart from my heart.
May they always dwell on my lips,
So the inclination of my soul

As well as the words of my mouth
May find favor in your presence,
My God and Sovereign.

4   *Six days shall you labor and do all your work, but
     the seventh day is a day of rest.*

If idleness is a vice,
Then constantly seeking out earthly possessions,
Dwelling on our problems and anxieties,
And spending all our efforts on material gain
Are no less fatal and destructive.
Our bodies would grow weary, our spirits
Would soon forget their heavenly mission on earth
And sacrifice their divine treasures for material gifts
If the Holy One had not graced us with the Sabbath
So we might refresh our bodies and direct our minds
Toward contemplation of the divine.
On that day, all shall take part in rejuvenating rest:
Parents and children, masters and servants;
Even the animals are included by the All-Loving God
In this commandment concerning the Sabbath:
God blessed the Sabbath day and hallowed it;
And it will become a blessing to us
If we sanctify ourselves with it
By ennobling meditations
And communion with our Protector and Creator.

5   *Honor your father and your mother.*

Our ancient sages remark,
Three beings have a share in each person:
God, Father, and Mother.
How sublime and sacred a child's duty must be
In the eyes of God, for its performance
Is summoned by a threefold voice:

By the feeling of filial love innate in our very beings;
By the law of thankfulness toward our parents,
Who are our guardian angels on earth
And have, after God, the greatest share in our beings;
And last, by the divine command,
Honor your father and mother, that all may go well with you.
Thus my sweet duty is three times blessed.
Father and Mother—oh, how my heart stirs for you
In love and gratitude. I will use all my power
To fulfill the divine command of a child's reverence
That resounds from every chord of my soul.

6   *You shall not murder.*

Our neighbor's life must be
A sacred, absolute good for us—
And not our neighbor's life alone but anything
That dignifies or elevates that person's life
Must not be violated or abused by us.
A sword or a dagger is not always required
To injure a heart.
A subtle, slanderous word can become
A poisonous arrow that wounds and kills.
Spiritual murder is no less destructive
Than a death blow struck by a murderer's hand,
Nor is it less punishable in the eyes of God.

7   *You shall not commit adultery.*

For a married couple the most sacred treasures,
The most priceless blessings,
Are love and faithfulness.
Who would dare destroy this crown,
Shred this wreath—who with cruel abandon
Would trample on these tender blossoms
That embellish another's matrimonial paradise?

Before the gates of this Eden, with boundless grace,
God has placed, like a cherub with a flaming sword,
A divine command: *You shall not commit adultery,*
So that every careless thought, every wayward emotion
Might be frightened off, to recoil in fear and trembling.

8   *You shall not steal.*

Let the thought never enter your mind
To take your neighbor's property for yourself.
Whether she may have acquired her possessions
Through her own labor
Or whether she may have become rich through
God's blessing alone, without any effort on her part,
Resolve never to lay your hand on what is hers.
Theft, whatever form or name it may assume—
Violence, fraud, or cunning—is always the same.
No matter how you may deprive your neighbor
Of what is hers, it will never save you,
And the blessings of God will flee from you.
You will have corrupted your hand
With a vulgar, base act;
And God—the Perfect, the Just, the Exalted One—
Will turn from you in anger.

9   *You shall not bear false witness.*

How much harm and evil
Do we cause in this world by false testimony?
Though we may not commit a crime
With our own hands,
We can still sustain it by speaking falsely in court—
And often, with a word, lead vice into victory,
Mislead judges to unjust decisions,
And oppress the innocent,
Who will cry out to God for revenge against us.

Perhaps we may think that the wrong we favor
Is not very great, may even be excusable;
But who can ever measure
The range that corruption may take?
Evil must beget evil, injustice must produce injustice.
Whenever we extend our hand to falsehood once,
It expands before we know it, increases in dimension,
Enmeshes us in its destructive net so we
Can never escape—and look!
To our horror we fall prey to its power.

10   *You shall not covet your neighbor's possessions.*

O Envy, source of all vices,
Whatever we possess as our own,
Whatever God's grace has provided for us,
You make appear small and insignificant in our eyes.
Only those things that belong to our neighbor
You present in shimmering beauty.
You direct our wishes to it and incite our desires.
You rob our heart of its peace,
Turn our life into a torment.
From the peace of a contented mind
You hurl us into the depths
Of discontent and discord with ourselves.
Therefore I will guard myself against envy,
Against coveting whatever belongs to another
And whatever God has judged well to deny me.

.   .   .

Praised are you, O Heavenly Parent, for these
Divine, pleasing, and saving doctrines and laws.
They are a priceless gift to us of your grace and truth.
We will hold them within our hearts, fasten them
To the doorposts of our house, bind them

To our arms and brows, that they may ever remain
Before our eyes and guide our lives,
So their light may open our eyes to truth,
Their admonitions strengthen us
In the performance of our duties,
And by pointing to you, Exalted One,
Cause us to find peace and consolation,
Enabling us to cheerfully and courageously
Stand up to the troubles and cares of earthly life.

Grant, O God, that the celebration of this festival
May sanctify my whole life
And make this a great and holy day—
A commemoration feast of your holy law,
Of your divine *Ten Words*. Amen.

DURING THE MONTH OF ELUL
אֱלוּל

Turn us to you, O ADONAI,
And we shall be turned;
Renew our days as of old.

—LAMENTATIONS 5:21

This final month of the year
Is full of serious and sublime significance for us,
For in these last weeks of the departing year
Our souls prepare themselves for that great day
On which you will sit in judgment over us—
You, Most Holy One, over us frail human beings,
You, before whom even the inhabitants of heaven
Cannot appear pure enough—how much less we,
With our weak, vacillating hearts,
Which are so often led astray consciously
Or unconsciously, and often deviate from you
And violate your holy laws.

Holy and blessed are these days to us
When, in our prayers and petitions,
We seek your pardon and forgiveness for our sins,
Which we are eager to wash away
With our repentance and our tears.
We long to return to you with true, sincere hearts
And with the firm resolve to mend our ways and habits.

Oh, may you sanctify these days for us
Through your blessings and grace.
All-Merciful God, Grant that they may become
Days of return and of reconciliation with you,
Days of true improvement and spiritual growth
In which our hearts may be opened
To renewed love for virtue and holiness.
May the quickening spirit of justice and peace
Enter our souls, inspiring us
To good and noble deeds, strengthened
For the struggle against weakness and harm.
May these days become days of fulfillment
For our prayers and petitions,
Days of pardon and forgiveness
For all our sins before you, Sovereign of All. Amen.

ON THE EVE OF THE NEW YEAR
עֶרֶב רֹאשׁ הַשָּׁנָה

Praise ADONAI, *O my soul;*
All that is within me, praise God's holy name.
Praise ADONAI, *O my soul,*
And do not forget all the good
God has done for you.

—PSALM 103:1–2

The day draws to a close, and with it
The outgoing year comes to an end
Like a sealed page—
A page to which we can no longer add,
A page from which we can no longer take.
It can be nothing for us now but a memory
That will serve as a witness for or against us.

In a cascade of images, the old year
Passes before my eyes. Once again

I see the shining moments of joy,
The blissful days and hours when your divine mercy
Enlightened me, when your rich blessings
Unfolded before me, and life showed me
Its most radiant aspect.
All those fortunate hours pass before me now,
Full of pleasure and contentment—all those times
When you blessed me with your goodness,
Those hours of useful action, in holy awareness
Of humanity's noble destiny and dignity.
My heart stirs and is filled with devotion.
My breast rises, overflowing with gratitude and praise
For you, Eternal Parent, ultimate giver of well-being.
Praise ADONAI, *O my soul;*
All that is within me, praise God's holy name.
Praise ADONAI, *O my soul,*
And do not forget all the good
God has done for you.

Yet gloomy pictures of the pain and struggle
I encountered—these also arise before me.
Some days I was troubled with fear and anxiety.
Some days brought bitter disappointments—
Hard tests that left my soul in mourning.
Sometimes danger and disaster
Confused and clouded my view.
Sometimes deep grief and heavy suffering
Oppressed my heart and drained my energy.
But even in those dark, bitter hours,
You allowed me to experience your love.
You brought my heart comfort.
When I was exhausted from the agony of trying,
You renewed and revived my strength.
When everyone else denied me help and rescue,
You reached out your hand to me just in time,
And when all others abandoned me,
You remained, all-loving, by my side.

Once more, my heart resonates with the deepest,
Most fervent song of thanks and love
For you, Eternal Parent.
Praise ADONAI, *O my soul,*
And do not forget all the good
God has done for you.

Night draws around us now,
And the old year comes to a close.
Almighty God, may this year end
With its afflictions and bitterness,
With all of life's worries and burdens:
Let all illness and frailty cease,
Let all disputes and discord fade away,
Let all hate and despair be lifted—
Let all the sins and transgressions that stain our lives
And that fill us now with regret and remorse
Be forgiven and forgotten in your sight.

With the first rosy glow of dawn
May we enter the new year
In a renewed, happier state of mind,
One that brings contentment and well-being
To us and to our loved ones—
Health and strength to our bodies,
Purity and good cheer to our souls,
Growth and prosperity to our children—
A blessed and productive year,
Untroubled and undisturbed in our enjoyment of it—
Peace and contentment to our hearts,
Peace upon our houses and our families,
Peace and blessing to our nation. Amen.

ON THE MORNING OF
THE NEW YEAR
שַׁחֲרִית לְרֹאשׁ הַשָּׁנָה

Like a maid's eyes to her mistress's hand,
So our eyes turn toward ADONAI, *our God,*
Awaiting favor.

—PSALM 123:2

As we concluded the old year
With tears and prayers before you, O God,
So we assemble again in the first hours of the new,
In your sanctuary, to dedicate our emotions to you
And open our hearts before your watchful eye.

O God, we ask so much of you for the new year!
As a child approaches a parent,
So we open our hearts and souls to you,
Confiding our joys and sorrows,

Our thoughts and feelings.
Whatever secret misery may depress us,
Whatever our souls may hesitate to bring to our lips,
The glowing tears in our eyes reveal
And our sighs and weeping lay bare before you.

But above all, this is what moves our souls:
We know that this is the Day of Remembrance.
Today the past year stands before you
Along with our deeds and works
To testify for or against us.
With fear and trembling we reconsider it.
With alarm we ask ourselves,
What will the past year testify about us?
Did we employ it for good and useful works?
Have we used these days for our eternal redemption,
For our ennoblement and improvement,
Or did we carelessly waste them in vain labors,
Merely to enjoy the short-lived fruits of life?
Did they vanish, therefore, like a dream,
Disappear like a cloud without value or importance,
Without gain or profit?

The year is gone forever, but the works,
Both good and evil, that we performed
Remain, and the recollection of our shortcomings
Weighs heavily on our souls, pierces our hearts
With sharp stings, covers us with shame and disgrace.
Only by deeply confiding
In your endless grace and mercy
Do we draw close to you this day, to absolve
With our sighs and tears
The heavy guilt that oppresses us.
Your compassion and kindness alone,
Which do not ask for the death of the sinner
But only that the sinner return and live,
Are my hope and consolation.

With humility and remorse
I call on your holy name, exclaiming:
Forgive, Creator of all human life—
Forgive my sins and deal with me
According to the measure of your mercy,
Which is great, and not according to my failures.
May you guard and protect me in the new year
As you have done to this day.
Preserve all those dear to me.
Inscribe us in the Book of Life for life,
For happiness, for well-being.
Remove all evil events, all sad destiny from us.
Cause the fruits of life to ripen before us
With mellowness and sweetness.
Cause the sun of your grace to illuminate our paths.
Grant the fullness of your divine blessing
To all our works, success to all our endeavors,
Satisfaction to all our labors,
Realization to all our hopes,
And fulfillment to all our wishes.
Wrap us truly and enduringly
In the blissful sash of peace and harmony.
Consider our grief with compassion;
Send healing to all the pains and wounds of our souls
As you do to the injuries and diseases of our bodies.
Send your help and consolation
To all who may need them.
Grant that we may patiently and openly
Accept all situations in life,
That we courageously and confidently
Look toward the future and walk before you
With pure hearts until, at the end of our days,
We appear before your heavenly throne
To deliver our account of them. Amen.

AT THE SOUNDING
OF THE SHOFAR
שׁוֹפָר

Save the people who know the sound of the shofar,
Who bask in your light, O ADONAI,
In the brilliance of your countenance.

—PSALM 89:16

How my heart stirs at the shofar's glorious blast.
Its vibration causes the very sinews of my being to echo.
Its earnest tones call out to me:
Mortal child, take courage! Take courage!
Another year has passed, yet you remain
Stained with old sins, weighed down
With past misdeeds and failings. Purify yourself!
Wash yourself in the waters of innocence.
Set your transgressions aside.
Through fervent hours of prayer to God,
With tears and remorse, shake off your old self.

Enter the threshold of this new year as a new being—
A new person made in the image of God,
A child imbued with innocence and a pure heart.
Enter the new year as a new being—
Made new in the capacity for all that is good and noble,
Made new in the firm intention and commitment
To serve God and to do good for your neighbors,
Made new in the sanctifying intent
To strive for freedom, truth, and justice.
As God has spoken:
Cast away all transgressions
By which you have transgressed,
And make yourselves a new heart and a new spirit,
That you may not perish, O House of Israel.

On this day, O God, you sit in judgment,
And the shofar's blast announces the judgment day.
The Eternal One, the holiest of all beings,
Stands in judgment over earth's weak child,
Born of dust, with sin clamoring at her heels.
God, you see all my secrets, count all my sins,
And I must pass before you!

And again the shofar sounds. In the midst of its call
The comforting thought comes to me that you, O God,
Are not only our judge, but also our parent.
You are not only all-just
But also all-merciful and all-compassionate.
You have created and established this awesome day,
This day of remembrance,
As an act of divine parental grace.
You have made it only for our healing and our blessing,
To call forth the human conscience and awaken it
From its passive slumber, from its pettiness,
From the ease of our daily lives and habits—
To shake us into an awareness of our better selves,

Our higher purpose on this earth.
With this thought, a comforting light strikes my soul
And I offer my prayerful and hopeful heart to you.

In tears I contemplate my sins
And deeply regret all my transgressions.
I pledge from this day forward
To pursue a better path and a purer life.
I pledge to you, O God, to transform myself:
With new love and a new eagerness,
I will heed your commandments,
Make your holy will one with my own,
And stand before you in humility and submission.

All-Merciful One, May my tears and my remorse,
My honest inner convictions,
Serve as effective advocates before your throne,
That you might look down on me
With forgiveness and compassion
And so free me from my guilt—
That I might begin the new year
As a pure and refined being,
Bringing me and my loved ones
Blessing and good fortune.
Let the shofar's evocative call
Echo within our beings all year long,
Reminding us of your all-seeing eye
And of Judgment Day, calling us
To act with virtue and to love goodness,
To overcome every harmful craving and desire,
As you overcome your anger
And clothe yourself in grace and mercy.

Save the people who know the sound of the shofar
And bask in your light, O God,
In the brilliance of your countenance. Amen.

MEDITATION FOR
THE DAYS OF AWE

In these sacred hours that you, O God,
Have set apart for our purification and atonement,
For our return to goodness,
For the communion of our spirits
With all that is heavenly and divine—
In these sacred hours
I unite all the energies of my being,
All the stirrings of my heart, all my wishes,
All my aspirations and capacities
In one firm thought, one unshakable resolve:
To abandon all evil inclinations
And allow myself to experience a rebirth
Of my heart's innocence and purity.

But, my God, will the inspiration
That glows within me here—in these sacred halls,
Where I feel your presence more than anywhere—
Will the enthusiasm that infuses me today,
When my ears are closed to all outside voices,
When I am cut off and separated

From all my connections to the outside world,
A day on which I am entirely absorbed
In the contemplation of your high, exalted being
And my own condition—
Will that enthusiasm and inspiration
Remain vivid to me when I leave this sanctuary
To return to the tumult of the outside world,
Where again I will contend with desire and sorrow,
Where the infatuating voice of material desires
Will resound in my ear or appear before me
In the dazzling form of fame and honor?

Aware of the heart's weaknesses and failures,
I tremble and fear that my good intentions
May again be shaken, that I may soon become
Faithless to my vows and resolutions.
Grant that the uplifting influences of this solemn day
May never be lost to me, that the virtuous spirit
That flows through me today may never vanish.
Grant that sin, in whatever form
And under whatever garb it may appear,
Be ugly and repulsive to my eyes
And, however alluring its flatteries may seem,
That I will always despise and flee from it
And instead always honor what is truly good
And acknowledge virtue in all its value and splendor.
May I always love and recognize the good
Whenever and wherever I meet it,
Even in the dwelling places of poverty and misery,
Even in the garments of want and weakness.
Oh, may I succeed in remaining strong, firm,
And steadfast in all good and noble endeavors.
May I become a better person
And aspire more and more toward you, my God,
So I may always be able to look up to you
With a clear conscience
And cheerful confidence. Amen.

ON THE EVE OF
THE DAY OF ATONEMENT
כָּל נִדְרֵי

"As I live," declares ADONAI,
"I will do to you just as you have spoken to me."

—NUMBERS 14:28

Most Holy One, in the midst of deep awe
At this most solemn hour
Our lips open to you in prayer—
At this hour that marks the beginning
Of the great Day of Atonement.
At this moment, your entire people
Rush toward their holy gathering places,
And our songs and prayers rise up to you
From contrite hearts.
Just as on the great Day of Judgment,
When those who have already returned
To the eternal journey of light
Stand at your heavenly throne,

So we all stand here today in your presence.
We lay open the book of our hearts,
Whose pages you read with all-seeing eyes,
Whose contents you regard with all-inclusive justice.
O God, even the angels of heaven
Are not pure before you.
We stand before you even less so,
Weighed down by guilt and aware of it.
Corruption dwells in our hearts,
And sin celebrates its triumph there.
Shouldn't we tremble before you?
Shouldn't our knees buckle and bend before you?

But you do not bring us here,
To this weighty recognition of our sins,
To break us down with guilt.
You do not bring us to this awareness
So we might falter in fear and anxiety
Before your anger,
Before the punishing hand of a strict judge.
You did not create this great, blessed day for that
But rather so you could, through it,
Bring back the despairing, the tired, the lost.
You created it so you could guide them again
To your loving heart, so you could make visible
For all who wander astray in the dark
The lights of your heavenly grace.
For this you have given us this day
And made it the holiest day of the year—
So we might, through solemn examination,
Through serious reflection on our inner lives,
Recover what so often eludes us
Amid life's demands and distractions
And what so often submerges
Under worldly pressures and influences:
Our better selves, our pious consciousness,
Our childlike hearts, our faithful way of being.

On this day the walls crumble
That separate the creations from the Creator,
That hold the innocent child far from the parent's heart,
The child's ear from the parent's word,
The child's gaze from the parent's loving face.
No matter how gravely we have sinned,
No matter how deeply we have fallen,
No matter how far we have strayed,
Your grace and mercy clear the higher path
So we might return again
To the community of the true and righteous.
We turn to you in remorse and repentance,
Trusting in your hallowed words:
And on this day, God will forgive you,
So you shall be cleansed of all your sins before God.

Eternal Parent, may my tears accomplish that.
May my fervent prayers rise toward you,
And may you receive them.
In your compassion
May you lift all guilt and sin from me,
And may your grace surround me
As in the earliest days of my innocence,
So my soul might be free and joyous,
So it might lift itself up to you
In holy awareness of your love and mercy,
So your protection might rest on me
And on all my loved ones. Amen.

ON THE MORNING OF
THE DAY OF ATONEMENT
מוּסָף לְיוֹם כִּפּוּר

The sacrifice God desires is a contrite spirit;
God, you will not despise
A humbled and broken heart.

—PSALM 51:19

With pain and melancholy, my heart calls up
Memories of the ancient Days of Atonement
That our ancestors observed
In your great temple in Jerusalem,
Where splendor and holiness alike
Poured out reflections of your glory and majesty
In hallowed chambers, where scores of Levitical priests
Performed your service amid celebratory song and chant
With joy and devotion, and where the high priest,
Brilliant in his heart's purity and in his splendor,
Entered before you to pray on behalf of his people,

Who stood gathered around him in humility and awe
To lay down their offerings upon your altar,
Where he made the blessed pronouncement:
On this day יהוה *will forgive you,*
So you shall be cleansed from all your sins
Before יהוה.

And the people, gripped with fear and trembling
From hearing God's holy name—
The most honored name, the awesome name—
How the mouth of the high priest,
In his holiness and purity, spoke it forth.
The people fell to their knees, bowed down,
Prostrated themselves, and cried:
"Praised be God's name, God's kingdom,
And God's holiness forever."
And as the temple service came to an end,
The high priest's face shone like the sun at midday,
Like God's holy angels on the heavenly throne,
For the people's offerings and prayers
Were pleasing to God and had been accepted with grace.
You forgave them, O Holy One.
The people stood pure before you once more.
The blots and stains of sin, once as red as blood,
Had been transformed in purity
To become as white as the moon.
Filled with joy and jubilation,
The entire congregation exulted before you
And threw themselves into joyful song.
Those who wandered the streets
Added their voices to the music.
They praised God with drums and harps,
And God's name became a festival of song.

This is how our ancestors
Celebrated the Day of Atonement.
Yet for us, none of this holiness has remained.

The consecrated state, the holy halls,
The blessed priests, the celebratory choir of Levites—
These are no more.
We have nothing but our fervent tears, our blood,
That we bring to you today in offering
Along with our fast and our regret.
With crushed and trembling hearts, we plead:
O Holy One, we have sinned before you.
We have transgressed—we and our entire household.
Oh, forgive us, Sovereign of All, our guilt
And our transgressions.
Take our regret, take our tears,
Take our pious words and resolutions as an offering.
Let the angels of your mercy and faithfulness
Be the ones who approach your throne on our behalf,
So that every blot may be taken from us,
So our guilt may be transformed into innocence,
So we may feel cleansed and forgiven, like newborns—
As at dawn, when night and fog disappear.
Let joy enter our hearts, along with jubilation
And the blissful awareness of God's forgiveness.
Let us find a new strength and capacity to be firm
In our hope in God, the one who never deludes us,
And in the joyous faith in God
That renews and revives the heart
Like a cool breeze in midsummer's heat,
So you may look down on us anew
With grace and tenderness,
And grant us all that the heart craves
At its innermost depths:
A year of blessing and prosperity,
Rich with fruits from the fields and gardens,
Rich with joyous, blessed events,
A year in which rest, joy, and peace
Reign in the land, a year in which
All our actions and undertakings are blessed.

Let well-being and cheerfulness
Spread throughout our homes.
Keep us far from suffering and calamity,
So we might take joy in God's gift of peace.
Let all who suffer be healed,
All who grieve be comforted,
Let all widows and orphans
Find caretakers and advocates,
And let all of our loved ones be sustained
For a long and happy life
That we might pursue your commandments
With tranquil, joyful, strong spirits and hearts,
That we may attach ourselves to your holy teachings
In constant love and faithfulness
Throughout our entire lives. Amen.

ON THE AFTERNOON OF
THE DAY OF ATONEMENT
מִנְחָה לְיוֹם כִּפּוּר

Their misdeeds have been all around them;
They have been ever before me.

—HOSEA 7:2

All-Compassionate One,
Our prayers rise toward you endlessly,
Seeking your forgiveness and acceptance
In repenting for our sins, which we regret
With our whole hearts and our entire souls.
Yet our regret is fruitless and comes to nothing
Unless it serves to watch and awaken
Our better selves, so we are not drawn again
Into the stream of temptations and errant pursuits.

May the regret within me today affect me so profoundly
That I remain far from sin and its sorry company,

That I strive for the good with all my strength,
And that I seek out and find examples of it
In all noble and worthy actions.

How many excellent models
Does the holy scripture offer
From our ancestors' lives—
From those great and righteous people
Who passed before you in unwavering devotion,
Whose lives we remember today
For forgiveness and mercy before you?
Isaac, the long-desired child of Abraham's old age,
The one whom Abraham led up at God's command
And lay down as an offering upon the altar without
Complaint, without lament, without question.
To God's call he answered: *Here I am!*

Oh, I feel it in the throbbing of my heart
When I think about my own child—
How Abraham must have choked at the thought
Of separating himself forever from his precious son.
In one single moment he lay down
All the wishes and hopes of a father's heart,
Laid them down upon the altar.
What can remain for an aged father,
Whose beloved child lies dead in his arms?
Yet without wavering or hesitation
He followed the voice of God
And led his son to sacrifice.

And Isaac himself, in the finest bloom of youth,
Accustomed to the love of his father,
Who had always carried him so gently;
Accustomed to the tenderness of his mother,
Who waited on his every heart's desire;
This well-favored boy, for whom the earth
And all of life must have been so marvelous—

Did not talk back, did not protest.
He was the lamb that God had chosen,
And that was enough for him
To offer his own neck
To the blade of the sacrificial knife.

What is greater or more worthy of our admiration
Than these exalted ones who were willing
To give of themselves to God with such devotion—
Abraham of his precious joy,
Isaac of his very life?
The spirit of love
That such a passionate devotion brings—
That is my goal, the pinnacle I strive to reach:
To offer my heart and soul to the Holy One.
Grant, O God, that I draw closer to this goal,
That I prevail in this aspiration,
That I let this conviction influence me for the good,
And that I practice this devotion
With all my thoughts and emotions,
With all my actions and deeds.

For only love makes a person strong enough
For this offering.
When I carry the love of God in my heart,
Then I can go steadily and willingly
Along all of God's paths, even when my tired feet
Must trod across dangerous cliffs,
Even when stones and thorns tear them to bleeding—
I will fulfill God's commandments with joy,
Even when their demands are difficult,
Even when they seem counter
To my worldly advantage and interests,
Even when they are opposed to my fondest desires.
For love is strong; love helps me persevere—
And when the Holy One calls for an offering,
I will exclaim with joy: *Here I am!*

And when that divine love inspires me toward others,
When it truly warms my innermost self,
When it raises and ennobles my heart,
I rush with joy to perform my next good deed.
I seek to ease my friend's suffering,
I reach out to dry her tears.
I cry with the unfortunate
And rejoice with the fortunate.
I take care to avoid injuring those around me
Or wronging them with harsh words
Or by casting blame.
I practice patience and kindness toward my neighbor.
I am compassionate to those in need,
I never close my hand to the poor or destitute.
With joy I bring myself to every opportunity
For charity and giving, and wherever it calls me,
I answer readily: *Here I am!*

How good is the life that takes its course
From the stream of such love.
Under its pure brilliance
All the heart's yearnings are transparent.
There goes sin, there go profane desires,
Until only the highest longings fill the heart and soul.
O Holy One, pour such a love into my heart.
Let such a love flow through me,
For you are the source and wellspring of all love. Amen.

THE REMEMBRANCE OF SOULS
יִזְכּוֹר

A human soul is ADONAI'*s lamp,*
Revealing a person's innermost being.

—PROVERBS 20:27

O Sovereign of All,
Ours is a deep, plaintive prayer
That we bring to you at this hour,
A prayer for the souls of our loved ones,
Whom death has called from our sides
And whom the earth has received.

A human life is fragile and fleeting,
Spare and impermanent in all that it has and holds.
It cannot be relied on, cannot support us.
It is not our luck, not our wisdom,
Not our brilliance, not our greatness.

At morning, we are honored and exalted;
At evening, we stand deep in the pit.
At morning, very fortunate;
At evening, broken down.
At morning, flush with vigor;
At evening, pale and dead.

Yet our trust and hope remain that we do not end,
That in death we do not cease to be.
Although earthly life passes away, another life begins—
A life that is nearer to you, O Eternal One,
A life of blessedness in your light.

Dust returns to the dust from which it came,
But the spirit returns to you, the one who granted it.
It lives before you and stays with you, O God,
Our refuge and our redeemer. There the soul
Reaches the goal it has struggled to achieve:
Rest for the aching heart, for the yearning spirit,
A sense of holiness and contentment.
There no pain can enter, no clamor, no shadow,
No cloud, no doubt, no despair.
There no cruelty pursues the innocent,
No violence attacks the defenseless weak,
No shadow darkens the inner gift,
No injustice embitters the noble heart.

There the dear ones who have gone before us reside.
There the enlightened spirit
Of [my beloved father, _____]
[And my beloved mother, _____] dwell(s).
With heartfelt love we recall them today
And pray for the rest and peace of their eternal souls.
Give them, O Holy One, a bright, high seat
In your heavenly realm, that all their sins
May be forgiven and any guilt be dismissed,

That they may live an everlasting
And holy existence in your presence,
Purified and cleansed, enlightened and hallowed
In the sight of your holiness
And in the brilliance of your divine nearness. Amen.

AT THE CLOSE OF
THE DAY OF ATONEMENT
נְעִילָה

As east is far from west,
So far has ADONAI
Removed our sins from us.

—PSALM 103:12

Almighty One, All-Compassionate One,
This holy day, which we have spent
In continuous repentance and self-reproach,
Striving for the cleansing and purification of our souls,
This holy day comes to an end.
Still once more we raise our pleading eyes to you,
And still once more we fervently
Cry out your name and praise you—
You who open the portals of compassion
To the repentant, returning sinner,

You who blot out our guilt
Through the strength of your mercy.

Oh, rejoice and be delighted, my soul!
For this day has released you
From the burden of sin's oppression.
The Holy One has cleansed you, forgiven you,
And uplifted you. The Eternal One
Has heard the pleading voices of our people.
God has accepted our fasts and self-reproach
And reached out a forgiving parental hand to us.
We entered this house as repentant sinners;
We leave it now as innocent children.

Grant, O God, that the purity and innocence of heart
That have been restored to us before you today
Never be lost to us.
May the noble feelings that arise within us now
Lead us through the course of our lives
And to life's end—so our souls may resemble
The way they were at the beginning
And leave this earth in purity and innocence—
To go and dwell with you
In the heavenly realm of eternity. Amen.

ON THE FIRST DAYS OF SUKKOT
סוכּות

You shall celebrate the festival of Sukkot for seven days.

—DEUTERONOMY 16:13

Once more the time has come for a festival.
So different from the last one,
Which we observed with tears and repentance,
With self-denial and confession,
This one we celebrate in joy, with jubilation
And with songs of praise, as it is written:
You shall rejoice before ADONAI, *your God,*
For seven days.
And how could good cheer and delight
Not resound through our hearts—how could holy joy
Not fill our souls after the Day of Atonement,
When you, O God, lifted our guilt from us
And set us free?

How, from the humble awareness of our darkest places,
Could a joyous ray of light beam so brilliantly
If you had not stretched out your forgiving hand?
You have not only forgiven us, you have also turned
Your countenance toward us again in love and kindness.
You do not pardon us as a lord might pardon a knight
But rather as a good parent gathers her regretful child
Into her arms, presses him to her heart,
And embraces him in love.
So you treat us, Eternal Parent,
In your vast, divine grace.
So we rejoice before you, my God.
With joyous, comforted spirits we enter the booths
We have built and decorated to honor your decree.
From our cleansed and renewed hearts
Our prayers rise up toward you.
We celebrate the festival of Sukkot in booths
Like a nomadic people, like our ancestors
Who lived in temporary shelters
As they wandered through the wilderness.
Elevated by wonder and blessed by your love,
Our ancestors pitched their tents on the open ground,
Yet your grace always surrounded them,
Protecting them from every enemy,
From every danger, from every need.
You were a pillar of cloud before them by day,
A pillar of fire beside them by night.
You made fresh water spout from rocks
To quench their thirst.
You sent down manna from the clouds to nourish them.
Their feet traveled unhurt across the burning ground.
Their balance did not fail. You led them
Until they entered the praised, promised land
That you had prepared for them as an inheritance.

Haven't you also worked wonders for us since?
Haven't you spread out your grace before us

As a shield and a cover for our hearts?
Haven't you spread your grace over your people,
So no enemy could bring them to shame?
For thousands of years
Israel has been a wandering people.
Our houses are but fragile huts—
And these have been torn asunder too many times
By unrest and the hatred of others.
We have only your mercy to thank
That we have not perished from the earth.
Your compassion has held us and carried us
Through storm and flood, over every abyss
That has threatened to devour us.
And now, after generations of wandering,
You have allowed us to taste the sweetness of home.
Thanks to you, we have found a homeland—
A beautiful, wonderful country
That recognizes us as its children.
Safe and free, like ancient Israel
In the shade of its palm and fig trees,
We rest beneath the tent of peace
Provided to us by the law,
Along with all our brothers and sisters in this land.

So we praise you, Eternal One, for the many wonders
You permitted our ancestors to witness,
And for the wonders you allow us, their children,
To witness even to this day. You have not
Forsaken us, and you shall never forsake us.
Praised and blessed be your holy name. Amen.

ON THE PROCESSION WITH
LULAV AND ETROG
לוּלָב וְאֶתְרוֹג

I wash my unblemished hands
And circle around your altar, O ADONAI.

—PSALM 26:6

Source of Being, how abundantly
You have adorned the natural world
With your gifts and blessings!
The valley with its luxurious greens,
The mountain with its crown of forests,
The fields with their fruits
Are all signs of your mercy,
Of your blessing to your human children
For the nourishment of their bodies
And the fulfillment of their needs,
For the delight of their eyes

And as a balm for their wounds.
Amid nature's vast richness
No leaf is too small, no blade of grass too humble
That it lacks healing power.
The simple shrub and the resplendent tree,
The sweet-smelling sprig and the golden fruit—
All of them call to us:
Praise, you mortal beings, the Almighty One,
Who created all these wonders.
Praise, you earthly children, your heavenly parent,
Who has provided and cared for you
With such abundant goodness.

So with praise, devotion, and gratitude,
We grasp this festival bouquet,
Which holds the fourfold signs of nature,
This miniature portrait
Of the rich diversity of the earth,
This declaration of your might and goodness, O God.
We raise, lower, and point it
Toward the six directions of earth and heaven
Because blessing awakens and sprouts
From all sides and corners of the universe.
Singing praises, we carry it around your altar.

Yet, Eternal One, not only do our mouths thank you,
Not only do our lips sing your praises,
But we also must honor and extol you
Through our deeds, through our devotion,
Through our love.
Just as you lovingly bless us with your goodness,
So shall we be loving toward the poor in our midst.
Just as you give us festivals of blessing and joy,
So shall we, through generous charity,
Bring joy and festive feelings
To the hearts of those who struggle.

This shall be our act of gratitude,
This our festival offering
That you accept in the fullness of your grace. Amen.

ON THE LAST DAYS OF SUKKOT

You shall rejoice in your festival.

—DEUTERONOMY 16:14

As we reach the last days of Sukkot,
Our hearts rise up to you, All-Compassionate One,
In gratitude for our joyous emotions
And for every beautiful festival experience
You have allowed us to share.

We have sat in our outdoor shelters
As you have commanded,
And we have eaten our festival meals within them,
Undisturbed and in good cheer.
With pious, celebratory feelings
We have sipped from your cup of joy,
And so we have praised and sanctified your name.

Soon we will leave these booths
And move back into our houses

Amid all the usual comforts of our lives;
There may you also spread
The canopy of your peace over us.
May you never let us forget that you alone
Are the foundation and pillars of our houses,
You alone are the support and umbrella of our lives,
You are the one who blesses the fields
And the wilderness, the home and the hearth.
You adorn our lives on this earth
With the gifts of your grace,
And when the *sukkah* of our lives and desires
Finally collapses, you open the portals
Of your heavenly home for us.

Our lives are truly like a *sukkah*.
Green, hopeful leaves make up its roof.
The walls are covered with ornaments and decoration.
The table is set with inviting, lovely treats.
Within it we experience a bounty of delights
As we gaze out on pleasant vistas of the natural world.
Yet often the sky grows dark,
And in the midst of our joyous feast,
In the midst of our celebrations,
A cold shower of misfortune rains down on our heads.
Heavy drops of bitter sorrow and pain descend on us.
The raw north wind blows
Through the fresh, cheerful walls of our *sukkah*,
And the partitions and poles
Of our luck and good fortune
Shake and shudder in the storm.
One festive flower after the next
Falls ragged beneath our feet.
One life ornament after another
Gets lost in the tumult.
Deep pain runs through our souls,
And we feel as if we've been delivered
To the unfairness of fate.

Then our only comfort is in remembering
That all of life is fleeting,
Like the festival of Sukkot.
Soon our earthly hut will break apart,
Our earthly husk fall away,
And our souls will return
To their eternal dwelling places.
We will leave all our earthly joys behind,
Those joys we so often take for granted.
They will remain behind, along with
All our earthly needs,
All our cares, sorrows, and worries.
All that will accompany us are our deeds and gifts—
All the labors of love we have practiced,
All we have offered and done
For good and noble purpose,
All the tears that thankful hearts
Have cried on our behalf—
These will be the garlands of gems
That decorate our heavenly dwelling places,
Ornaments that never spoil and never pass away.
There our hopes will ripen into glorious fruition,
Our merits blossom into crowns,
And all our suffering transform into endless joy.

Let us be mindful of all this, O God,
That it might serve as a good teaching and healing
Throughout the course of our lives,
So we never let ourselves be crushed
By misfortune's heavy hand,
Never let ourselves be carried away
By the dazzle of good fortune,
Never forsake the holy treasure of our eternal beings
For the sake of adorning our flimsy, earthly huts.
Let our lives be wholesome, holy,
God-pleasing lives before you now and forever. Amen.

ON THE FESTIVAL OF
REJOICING IN THE TORAH
שִׂמְחַת תּוֹרָה

ADONAI's commandment is brilliant,
Enlightening the eyes.

—PSALM 19:9

Today we celebrate a sublime festival of joy,
The sacred feast of faith and the divine law.
With delight and love, we listen
To the concluding words of the Torah.
With delight and love we greet it
As we swing open its doors again.
This is the Torah that blesses us
With the richness of heavenly joys
And makes us truly happy.
It is the tree of life, whose fruits
Nourish the eternal spirit
And rejoice the pious soul.

It is the banner around which
All the pious gather and beneath which
All true believers join hands in holy covenant.
It is the standard on which they swear to perform
All that is good, holy, and for the honor of God
And the glorification of their tradition.
It is the cup from which we drink
Peace and tranquility for the afflicted soul,
Renewed hope and sweet faith for the drooping spirit,
Heavenly comfort and a healing balm
For the lacerated heart.
It is the sun that illumines the earth's dark valleys.
It is the light that cheers the gloomy huts
Of misery and misfortune
And makes them shine with pure joy in God.

Thanks to you, O God,
For entrusting such a jewel to us.
We adore and worship you for enriching us
And enhancing our lives through your Torah.
Without it, our life would be a barren, fearsome dream,
A small boat without a guide on a stormy ocean.
I shudder to think of where I would be without it.
Sacred exultation moves my soul when I recall
What a treasure I possess in it.
Grant, Almighty One, that your divine word
May ever be alive within me,
That it may ennoble and fortify my heart,
That it may strengthen my faith, my love,
My hope in you through suffering and hardship
And in all the trials and calls to courage
I may encounter on my way.
May the blessings of your word never leave my home
Or those of my children and my children's children.
May the brilliant rays of your heavenly peace and joy
Always inspire and cheer me. Amen.

ON HANUKKAH
חֲנוּכָּה

O God, what can I say now that Israel
Has bared its neck to its enemies?

—JOSHUA 7:8

My God and Sovereign, The lights shimmer
So cheerfully in our houses tonight—
These lights that we kindle as evening falls,
Their gentle glow recalling the time
When your merciful light shone down on us
In the midst of a night of oppression and danger.

As the terrifying hand of King Antiochus was raised
Against your people, as it oppressed us and abused us,
As the Syrian king, in his stubborn frenzy,
Tried to compel us to deny our faith
And turn our wholesome honor of God into idolatry—

As he desecrated the temple
And disgraced the holy tabernacle,
You called forth mighty, glorious warriors
And champions of right from among your people.
You set up the noble sons of Mattathias
At the head of that small band of Maccabees
And lent them victory and triumph.
Then our ancestors came into your temple,
Purified the holy spaces
That the barbarians had desecrated,
Kindled the lights at the holy places,
And dedicated this day
As a day of liberty and celebration for all time.

In the shimmer of these lights we remember those days
When absolute faith and childlike love of you,
Exalted Eternal One, returned again
To the faltering, weary hearts of your people,
When our holy religion inspired their hearts once more
And burned within them
With heavenly strength and purity
In all its shining nobility.

May these little lights,
Which serve as a testament to that great epoch,
Also beckon us to rekindle the holiest awe, love,
And trust in you, Eternal Parent, in our own hearts.
May we always nurture these holy feelings,
So we do not grow weary or falter
When misfortune and trouble enter our lives.
And when we are faced with difficult tests,
May we honor your will with dedication and piety,
Patiently bearing whatever we have been given,
Never crying out in doubt,
"There is no help for us in God."
You place burdens on us

And you relieve us of our burdens,
You change darkness into light and mourning into joy.
May you make our hearts strong and vigorous,
That we may always act with complete devotion
And firm commitment to you and your holy word,
Proving ourselves to be courageous warriors
And champions of your divine command. Amen.

ON PURIM
פוּרִים

The Jewish people had light and gladness,
And joy and honor.

—ESTHER 8:16

Jubilation and joy fill the hearts of your people today,
My refuge and my protector.
Our souls overflow with gratitude
On this festival day and day of remembrance
For our rescue and deliverance from beneath the hand
That had spun out such a dreadful plan
For the people of Israel.
It was not slavery that would have been our lot,
For even in slavery hope remains of eventual freedom.
It was not poverty and need
That would have oppressed us,
For in time even that destiny often reverses itself

Until blessing and abundance replace hardship.
Instead we would have been annihilated—
Torn entirely from life and erased,
Along with all our hopes and expectations.
The future for Israel would have been no more.
With one strike
The entire tree might have been severed
From crown to root, from bough to branch.
Yet you, rescuer of the oppressed,
You, protector of the pursued,
You heard the cries of your people for help,
The cries of their pounding, frightened hearts.
You sent rescue and redemption,
Transformed their mourning into joy, death into life,
Lamentation and shame into honor and exaltation.
You allowed the plans of the godless Haman
To fall back on his own body;
The pit he'd dug for us swallowed him up instead,
And the passionate words of extermination
He had spoken against the Jewish people
Devoured him and his entire heritage.

And through whom did you accomplish
This great and wonderful deliverance?
You, O God, chose a young woman for your messenger,
For an instrument of your people's redemption,
That all the world might learn
How great you are also in little things,
How your power works also in gentleness,
How that which seems powerless
Turns triumphant and mighty in your hand,
And how that which is tender and humble
Is revealed to be strong and sublime.
Through your miraculous redemption
We may also know and accept wholeheartedly
That no matter how modest our means,

We are nevertheless commissioned by you
To do good for the benefit and blessing of others.

O God, also grant that whatever powers
You have given me
May help me to perform good and useful deeds,
That my life may not pass away
Without having borne fruit,
And that my name may be worthy
To be praised and blessed
By those who live with me
And by those who shall live after me. Amen.

4

PRAYERS ESPECIALLY FOR WOMEN

A DAUGHTER'S PRAYER
FOR HER PARENTS

Honor your father and mother
That your days may be long on this earth
That ADONAI, *your God, has given you.*

—EXODUS 20:12

My God and Sovereign, you are the source
Of the highest, purest, and holiest love.
You look graciously down on all sincere love,
But what feeling of love on earth is purer and holier
Than a child's love for her parents?
You alone have made it holy, have placed it in our hearts
And have commanded us to honor and revere
Our fathers and mothers,
That our days may be long on this earth.
And for them—the earthly representatives
Of your endless, heavenly love—

My fervent prayer now ascends to you
From the depths of my heart.

O God, preserve my dear parents,
Preserve for me these guardian angels of my existence,
Those founders of my happiness,
The greatest benefactors of my life
To whom I owe so much,
To whom I am so indebted.
They have nursed me and attended to me,
They have guided and taught me,
They have watched over and cared for me,
They have labored and struggled for me
With their hearts' blood
And brought me up and instructed me
To know you, my God,
And to direct my heart to you in love and confidence.
Led by their loving hands
I passed through my bright infancy
As if through a beautiful, fragrant garden
Full of sweet blossoms and flowers.
Every thorn and stone was removed from my path
By their love and concern.
In all the events in my life
I always found the best consolation,
The most tender sympathy with them.
I seek in vain to find the words to convey
The ardent and profound emotions that move me,
But you, O God, look into a person's innermost being.
The most secret feeling speaks to you,
Searcher of Innerness,
And this deeper language reaches you,
Though my mouth may lack the words
To convey them to you. Oh, may you grant
Your gracious fulfillment of my wishes
And may you bless my beloved parents

With your best, most beautiful, and richest gift—
A long and peaceful life—and please them
With all the joys and delights of earthly existence.
May you make their old age full of gladness,
Free from care and pain. May you satisfy
All the elevating hopes that fill their loving hearts,
Through us, their children. Oh, may this be
Your holy will, Heavenly Protector. Amen.

A DAUGHTER'S PRAYER FOR HER ADOPTIVE PARENTS

Those who decide justly should be pleasant,
And a good blessing will come upon them.

—PROVERBS 24:25

God, eternal source of all goodness and mercy,
In whose hand rests reward
For all that is noble and charitable on earth—
You who bestow your rich store of blessings
On those who perform deeds of charity and love—
I come to you, my heart filled with thanks,
To pray for the well-being and redemption
Of my adoptive parents,
For those noble and good people
Who have devoted such kindness and love to me,
Who have made such sacrifices on my behalf.
They did not conceive me nor give birth to me,

They did not bear me beneath their hearts,
And I am not their flesh and blood. Nonetheless,
They have assumed the duties
Of father and mother to me.
They have nourished and cared for me;
They have raised and guided me toward all that is good.

O All-Compassionate One, bestow goodness on them
With the entire fullness of your divine parental heart.
Take them under your protection
Just as they have taken me under theirs.
Surround them with your grace
Just as their love and kindness has surrounded me.
Let a long and fortunate life be their portion,
And let them fully enjoy and savor
All the joys and delights of being.

Heavenly Parent, be charitable
To a daughter's prayer for them.
Purify my feelings and illuminate my understanding
That I may, through all my feelings, thoughts,
And actions, express my gratitude toward them.
May I, through a pious and humble course of life,
Become ever more worthy of their goodness toward me,
And may I, through diligent labor and ambition,
Through noble expression in word and deed,
Demonstrate the love and virtue they have shown—
Making it clear to all—and may I satisfy
All the hopes and dreams they have for me. Amen.

FOR AN ORPHAN

Even if my father and mother
Had forsaken me,
ADONAI *would still take me up.*

—PSALM 27:10

God, my God! All your creations
Call out your name in heartfelt prayer.
How earnestly my heart rushes toward you.
My soul fervently loves and longs for you,
For I stand lonely and forlorn on earth.
Heavenly Parent, my hope, trust, and future
Rest in you alone.
Those whom I thank for my life,
Those whose love shielded and guided my youth,
Have been called back to you in your luminous heaven,
And I am left alone and orphaned on this dim earth.
Here, where there are so many cliffs

And stumbling blocks that I, in my inexperience,
Do not know how to sidestep;
Here, where there are so many burdens
That I, in my vulnerability, am not able to withstand;
Here, where there are so many struggles
To which I succumb in my weakness.
May you, refuge for the oppressed,
Protector of orphans,
Never let your parental loyalty or love for me falter.

O Parent of All, please do not forsake me!
When I am in need of counsel and help,
Let your counsel and your help be my portion.
When danger surrounds me,
When trivial enticements addle my good sense
And captivate me, then, All-Compassionate One,
Let me hear your warning and your saving voice;
Let your words wake me out of my giddiness.
And when my heart is filled with longing and dismay,
Then, my God, let me feel your nearness.
Let comfort's gentle dew filter into my faltering heart.
Teach me to have faith
That I will never be forsaken or alone,
That your hand guides me through life,
That you will help me carry life's troubles and burdens,
That you will care for me, that you protect me,
That your love always surrounds me.
Grant, All-Compassionate One,
That my life may please you.
Let the aspiration toward goodness arise within me.
Let my entire consciousness be filled with it,
So that no sinful doubts or immoral musings
May find room in it or ground in which to grow.
Let my days pass in purity and innocence of heart.
Let my mind be firmly impressed with the knowledge
That only through upright and virtuous conduct

Can I honor my parents in heaven,
And only on the path of awe before God
Can I attain the blessedness of eventually being
Reunited with them in the realms of the eternal.
Bless, All-Compassionate One,
All those who lighten my burden
Through their kindness and good deeds.
Teach me, through modesty and humility,
Through a wise and pleasant demeanor,
To win the hearts of those around me,
And may you, my Creator,
Always find me pleasing in your sight
And in the sight of others. Amen.

FOR A BRIDE
ON HER WEDDING DAY

Let me kiss my father and mother good-bye,
And then I will follow you.

—I KINGS 19:20

All-Good God, soon I shall come close to you,
At the side of the one you have sent
To be my life's companion.
The solemn moment is fast approaching
That will forever unite me with my beloved.
Oh, how my heart throbs—
How it pulses between fear and hope!
For I know the importance
And solemnity of this moment.
I know that from now on
My life will assume another form,
That I am accepting new, sacred duties

That are often difficult to fulfill,
And that the life I am about to enter
Will be uneven and uncertain.
Therefore I pray to you from the depths of my heart—
Please assist me!
Be my guide, shield, and protector on all my pathways.
Grant that I may remain united
With my life's companion
In unceasing fidelity and undisturbed harmony.
Turn our destinies into blessings,
Guard us against all trials and tribulations,
Strengthen me
So I might be a good and faithful wife to him.
Make the days of our life together
Days of happiness, tranquility, and ease,
Sacred joy and mutual contentment.

O God, hear my prayer!
Crown us with your blessing,
So with joyful, happy hearts,
We might look back on this solemn day
And remember you with gratitude.
Fulfill for me the consoling promise,
God grants your heart's desire
And fulfills all your wishes. Amen.

FOR A NEW BRIDE

The wisest of women builds her house,
But the foolish one tears it down with her hands.

—PROVERBS 14:1

All-Compassionate Sovereign,
Governor of all human history,
I have looked to you all the days of my life, yet
Even more so, my God,
Do I take refuge in you today,
For I stand at the brink of a new epoch in my life,
When new emotions and wishes enter my heart
And open me up to new purpose and responsibilities.
I am wedded to a man and have promised him
My love, fidelity, and devotion for a lifetime,
To be his loving companion in joy and in sorrow,
A faithful and constant life partner
In the building of our home and our future.

My God, may you bless the betrothal of our hearts.
May you bring together within me
Those feelings, affections, and life perspectives
That are the mother of all respect and harmony.
May you let love's healing, life-giving sun
Shine on our horizons—a sun that, in its radiance,
Warms and illuminates all of life's
Landscapes and horizons, clarifies
Good fortune's pinnacles with its brilliance,
And raises up misfortune's depths
With its penetrating rays.
The higher we climb toward heaven
The greater the strength and warmth we receive
To produce blossoms and fruits, and to ripen.

All-Compassionate One, may you illuminate my spirit
So I might prepare myself well
For the responsibilities that await me,
That I will learn with diligence and eagerness
To undertake everything necessary
For our well-being and happiness
And to express my true desire to become
A worthy and wise life partner for my husband,
To grow with him, taking joy in his happiness,
And abandoning any superficial vanities
That might enthrall a young woman.
Instead, let me adopt a warm spirit of graciousness;
Let me give up any rash, childish impatience
And joyfully allow a spirit of gentleness and serenity,
Forgiveness and acceptance, to enter my heart.
I ask your protection, All-Compassionate One.
I place my hope in your strength and your help.
May your mercy and grace shelter me forever. Amen.

FOR AN EXPECTANT MOTHER

To the woman, God said,
"I will let your pangs be great in childbearing;
In pain shall you bear children."

—GENESIS 3:16

O Almighty One—the one from whom life comes,
From whom the strength for life
And the joy of life arises—
You have been mindful of me
And have given me this sweet joy:
The prospect of becoming a mother.
Beneath my heart, I feel the seed of a new life
That shall, through me, come to see
The light of the world—
My husband's child and mine,
A new being born of our wedded joy,
A new bond born of our wedded love.

Parent of All, I thank you
For having given me, your servant,
The blessing of motherhood.

In your wisdom you have spoken the ominous words,
I will let your pangs be great in childbearing;
In pain shall you bear children.
Should we be permitted to mutter and complain
That you, in your great goodness,
Imposed this on us?
Wise and good are all your decrees.
For long months you allow our unborn children
To rest beneath our hearts until they ripen into life,
Allowing us a period to prepare
For the great and weighty obligations of motherhood,
Allowing us to gain the knowledge and insight
That we still lack in taking up this task.
You have coupled this time with pangs and pains
Because every pain, every discomfort we feel,
Should remind us that we are becoming mothers,
Should guide the soul to recall
The exalted task and decree that we are accepting.
And why shouldn't we gladly bear the fleeting pangs
And joyfully carry this blessed burden?
Why shouldn't we gladly forgo
Some comforts and pleasures
And accept some sacrifices
For the sweet and fulfilling experience of motherhood,
For the good fortune and blessing of having children?
Our children shall be
As fruit-bearing trees in God's orchard,
For God is the one who allows us
To continue to blossom through our children,
The one who makes us so rich and fortunate
Through the precious treasures
Of a child's love and loyalty.

Parent of All, may you allow the tender fruit within me
To thrive and ripen into a perfect, healthy child,
And bless this child with a strong body
And a beautiful, pious soul.
Grant me also the constancy, discretion, and restraint
To refrain from anything that might harm or endanger
My unborn child, that I might always be aware of it
And guard myself against damaging influences,
Never allowing myself to become overwhelmed
By fear, anger, grief, sorrow,
Or anything else that agitates and disturbs
The soul's tranquility.
May you hear me, O God, my refuge,
In whom I hope and trust. Amen.

ON THE APPROACH
OF CHILDBIRTH

Before she labored, she was delivered;
Before her pangs came, she bore a son!

—ISAIAH 66:7

Fear not, worm of Jacob,
O people of Israel,
For I will help you.

—ISAIAH 41:14

The hard, painful hour of delivery draws near,
And in the midst of the pains and fears
That course through me
This fervent prayer rises from the depths of my soul—
May it ascend to you, Eternal Parent!
With every pain, with every pang that seizes me,
My words die on my lips.

Only your name, my God, remains alive on them.
They utter this cry alone: *God, my God!*
You who are my shield and my protector,
My comfort and my rescue,
The one who dampens my fears and my fright,
The one who embraces me in hope,
The one who is my strength—
Oh, as I raise my tearful eyes up to you, Parent of All,
May it draw your compassion down to me.

Let your mercy shelter me,
So these birth pangs do not overtake me,
So I am able to bear them with courage and strength.
Oh, that your parental grace
Might guide me safely and securely
Across this awesome threshold.
All-Compassionate One, shorten my suffering.
Let me soon achieve the joyous goal of this labor—
Let me soon enjoy a healthy, strong baby.
My God, do not now recall
All my sins and missteps in life!
Forgive me and pardon me now
For all my failings before you.
In your compassion and mercy, may it be your will
That I give life to a precious new being.
Preserve my life, and be with me,
For all my hope and trust rests in you. Amen.

AFTER A SAFE DELIVERY

For a child has been born to us,
A child has been given.

—ISAIAH 9:5

All-Compassionate One, Your divine help
Has ushered me through the hour of delivery,
The hour that loomed before me for so many months,
An hour marked by such pain and suffering,
Such fear and danger.
Your mercy has held and carried me.
Your presence has supported and strengthened me.
Now this process has brought its joyous outcome.
I am alive, and at my side rests
My beloved, painfully acquired infant—
This dear, sweet, beautiful child!
Almighty One, my murmuring lips are soft and weak,
But my heart speaks to you with such strength and zeal.

Parent of All, I thank you!
I am so profoundly grateful for your merciful guidance,
For all the good and joy I have received from you.
A still, holy, divine bliss courses through my soul.
It fills my heart with joyous hope in you, my God—
You who have guided me so mercifully
Across the cliffs and rocky terrains of life.
To you I entrust my life and future.
To you I commend the life and future of my child.

I ask only that you never withdraw your love from me.
Grant me the wisdom and strength
To fulfill my maternal obligations to the utmost degree
And according to your will.
Let everything that comes to my child
Be for the development of [his/her] body and spirit.
Let me guide my child with prudent awareness
On the path of goodness and truth,
That I might teach [him/her]
To recognize and love virtue,
As well as to honor and pray to you, my God,
Throughout the entire course of my child's life. Amen.

ON RETURNING TO SYNAGOGUE
AFTER CHILDBIRTH

Even the bird finds its house again
And the swallow its own nest
Where it had sheltered its young:
Your altars, O ADONAI,
My Sovereign and my God.

—PSALM 84:4

Blessed is the hour when I reenter your sanctuary,
Where I may again open my heart
To my God and deliverer
Within a community of worshipers.
Almighty God—here, where so many hearts
Open in unison to adore and glorify your name,
Also accept my thanks and praise.
May my deep emotions, my sincere prayer of gratitude
Be as acceptable in your sight as the sacrifices

That pious mothers once offered you in days past.
On the altar of my heart I will sacrifice
All vain and empty desires and wishes,
And here in your holy temple, at this precious hour,
With my soul overflowing with love,
I pledge my life to you, giver of life and redemption.
I pledge before you and before myself
To unite all my powers and capacities
To fulfill my responsibilities
As a Jewish wife and mother
And to devote my heart and soul to these pursuits
All the days of my life.

Almighty God, graciously accept my vows
And grant me your blessing, that I may never falter
In fulfilling them, that I might always find
Pleasure and gratification in achieving them,
And that I shall continue to find
More delight in doing good
Than in any other earthly pleasure.
Grant me the wisdom and strength
To educate my children
To become good and noble people;
Honest, useful citizens; and sincere, observant Jews.
Bless my husband that he may live a long, healthy life,
That his labors and hard work for our children
May always be crowned with success
And that we may never find ourselves in want.
Bless our children, that they may grow and thrive
In soul and body, that they may become
The pride and joy of our hearts and find favor
In the eyes of God and of the world. Amen.

FOR A CHILDLESS WIFE

ADONAI is mindful of us.
God will bless us;
God will bless the House of Israel,
God will bless the House of Aaron.

—PSALM 115:12

All-Gracious God, you have created
All that lives and moves in this great world
That it may continue from generation to generation,
All colored by the contented awareness
Of having fulfilled its duty.
With joy a mother lifts her child to her breast.
Smiling beneath her tears, she forgets all her worries,
Her pain, her life's struggles,
And is filled with the strength and courage
To enjoy the pleasures of motherhood
And to provide motherly love.

Even the wild beast, fondling its young, seems tame
As it bears and protects, guards and nourishes its young,
Yet she would defend them with her own blood.
Even the seed-bearing plant shakes its head in the air
With confidence, broadcasting its seeds far and wide
That they might spring up a thousandfold from the soil.

But I—I do not know these joys.
I know them only by sight, but alas
Not through my own experiences.
You, Almighty One, have not seen fit
To grant me these maternal pleasures
And have denied me the happiness
Of calling a child my own—
Refused me that sweet bond
That unites the hearts of husband and wife
In harmony and love and, with its very breath,
Extinguishes the flame of discord between them
And causes peace to enter their home.
When cold, blossomless old age arrives
And their hearts could very well shrink,
Their child appears like a twig in full bloom,
And with the fresh love and warm life
Their offspring brings, they grow young again.

As Hannah, a childless wife, poured out
Her heavy sadness, her wishes and hopes
In heartfelt prayer before you,
So do I stand before you, O my God,
In the fullness of my grief and sorrow,
And pray that you may hear my petition
As you once fulfilled her supplication.
Oh, may the tree of my life bear sweet blossoms,
May my house be filled with the joy of children,
May my conjugal life be adorned
With the blessing of offspring.

But if you, in your inscrutable wisdom,
Have so ordained to leave me childless,
Then, O Source of Being, I longingly beg of you
To grant me the strength and courage
To reign my wishes to your exalted will,
Accept your judgment with humility,
And always remember that your redemption comes
Not only from what you give us
But also from what you refuse.
May I also always remember
That although you may have denied me
A mother's joy, you have already granted me,
In your endless goodness, countless pleasures
And will surely grant me more each day.
May I always remember that although a mother's tasks
Are not among my duties,
My life is not without its use and value,
And that many other no less sacred and satisfying tasks
Are bound up in my existence: to be a loving wife,
To be a mother to the needy and the oppressed,
To be a mother to the lonely orphan.
May I devote all my energies to these sublime purposes
And thereby seek and find my joy and comfort.
May this be your divine will. Amen.

ON THE CIRCUMCISION OF A SON

I said to you, "In your blood you shall live."

—EZEKIEL 16:6

I thank and praise you, All-Compassionate One.
In your mercy, you have blessed me with a son
Who will be taken up today
Into the holy covenant of our faith.
With a joyous heart, I dedicate him to you,
And with joy and holy emotion I affirm
That the blessed covenant you crafted with our people
Shall be marked upon his body.
With his blood it shall be sealed.
May this be a pleasing offering to you.
May the blood that flows out of his tender body today
And every cry of pain that rings from his infant heart
Rise to you like a dedicated prayer:
That your mercy should surround him for his entire life,

That he find pleasantness with you, O God,
And favor in the world,
That he be able to achieve everything he undertakes,
That everything he begins be for a blessing.
Before *all else* and above *all else*, Almighty One,
Strengthen him in body and spirit,
That he be strong in his faith,
Strong in virtue and piety,
That he gladly offer up
The pleasures and comforts of life
To make the higher, divine will his own,
That he surrender the wishes and cravings
Of his own heart, All-Merciful One,
To fulfill your wishes and commandments.
As today his blood is spilled on the altar of faith,
May he later in life also be prepared to offer
That which is most precious to him
For the memory of the pious and the holy,
For the glory and redemption
Of his people and his faith,
For the well-being and deliverance of humanity,
And for the honor and sanctification
Of your great name. Amen.

ON THE NAMING OF A DAUGHTER

A good name is better than good oil.

—ECCLESIASTES 7:1

Praised be you, O God—
You who show your mercy in so many ways.
You place emotion so sweet and cherished
In a woman's heart that nothing can outweigh it.
This emotion is so great and uplifting
That, through it, she feels nobler and worthier
In her own eyes and in the eyes of others.
Motherly love and motherly dignity—
These can be the source of so many virtues,
They can drive out all petty and vain concerns,
Harmful habits and pursuits.

I exalt and praise you, my God, for you have blessed me
With these precious feelings, too.

You have given me a daughter,
Whom I will always carry in my heart
With affection and love,
Whose care and raising you have entrusted to me.
As I witness her tender growth
I will experience once more with joy
My own childhood and youth.

Today, for the first time, she receives
The blessing of our religion.
May your blessing, O God,
Rest upon her now and always.
Today she receives a name in your holy presence.
May she, through a pious, wholesome course of life,
Make it a worthy and noble name.
All-Compassionate One, may this name
Be written in your merciful Book of Life
For life and good fortune.
May she be equal in stature to our pious mothers
Sarah, Rebecca, Rachel, and Leah—
Blessed and hallowed with all the virtues
Of life and trust in you;
Tender and generous, devout in her faith,
Modest, loyal, and giving; a good daughter,
A young woman of winning spirit and heart,
An honest wife and virtuous mother
On whom rests the blessing of heaven
And the high regard of her fellow human beings. Amen.

FOR THE MOTHER OF
A BAR/BAT MITZVAH

בַּר־מִצְוָה / בַּת־מִצְוָה

This is the child I prayed for.
And ADONAI *has granted my request.*
In turn I hereby dedicate him to ADONAI—
For as long as he lives he is dedicated to ADONAI.

—I SAMUEL 1:27–28

All-Gracious God, I thank you
For allowing me to reach this day—
A day of thanks to you, a day of feast and joy to me.
You have allowed me to educate and guide my child
With a mother's love and tenderness,
To provide my child with all [he/she] needs,
And to prepare my child for the solemn act
Of this day on which [he/she] is received
Into the congregation of the faithful

To be a member of your people and your covenant,
To participate in the performance and fulfillment
Of your holy laws and statutes.
Gratitude and praises to you, O God,
For your grace and compassion.

Oh, please also grant your grace and mercy to my child.
May the light of Torah, this gladdening boon of heaven
To which my child dedicates [himself/herself] today,
Ever fill [his/her] entire being, that [his/her] soul
May be illuminated by the lamp of truth,
[His/her] heart be inspired
Toward all that is noble and great,
And [his/her] spirit strengthened and encouraged
For every struggle [he/she] may encounter.
May love for you permeate and inspire my child
All the days of [his/her] life,
That [he/she] may cleave to you
With [his/her] whole heart
And with [his/her] whole might.

O Holy One, please be present
Within my child's deepest being,
That it may become a pure, consecrated temple to you.
Grant that this tender child may grow up and mature
To be a strong instrument of redemption
For our people and community, to glorify our faith
And promote all that is good and useful on earth.

Hear, O God, the fervent prayer of a mother's heart.
Strengthen my child's body, let [his/her] strength grow
And [his/her] understanding mature.
Let all that is within [him/her] develop and advance
Yet still preserve the purity of [his/her] mind,
The innocence of [his/her] soul,
And the peace of [his/her] heart

As they now fill [his/her] youthful being.
May my child remain yours throughout [his/her] life
A lamb that you will never cause to want,
That you will lead through green pastures,
Beside fresh, quickening waters.

And as for me, O God, grant me also now,
And for a long time to come, the happiness
Of watching over my child and delighting in [him/her]
With the grace and gratification
Of a mother's love. Amen.

A MOTHER'S PRAYER FOR THE SUCCESS OF HER CHILDREN

A wise son is a father's joy;
A foolish son is a mother's sorrow.

—PROVERBS 10:1

All-Compassionate One, *children are*
Gifts of your mercy and the reward for virtue.
A praiseworthy child—
How a mother's heart beats with exaltation
At the sound of those words.
Successful children are the flowers
That make our lives a Garden of Eden.
They are the sweetest fruits of our life's tree,
The holy tributes we leave behind us on this earth;
Their pious prayers serve us even in the afterlife.

Successful children are gifts of your grace,
But how awful, my God, when they fail!

A mother's life is devoted
To the care and raising of her children.
Her heart and mind dwell on them—
On all they do and all they strive to do.
To help them prosper, no sacrifice is too great for her,
No effort too heavy. When they fail,
Her entire life is disrupted.
All cheerfulness, all joy lie buried
Beneath heavy clouds of sorrow, darkening her hopes.
For *a wise child is a father's joy,*
But the one who fails is a mother's distress.
O dear God, may your grace protect me from this pain.
In addition to the keen awareness of my misfortune,
I must also add the heartrending thought
That I may not have fulfilled my maternal duties.

Sometimes in a child's nature,
In the child's physical or mental constitution,
An unfortunate impairment or injury exists,
Yet through wise and attentive care and upbringing,
It is often possible to strengthen a sickly plant
And raise it into a hearty, strong, and healthy shoot;
But through neglect or error,
Through weakness or ignorance,
Instead of healing the brokenness,
We may instead increase and magnify it.
With our own hands, we may guide our children
Into ruin. With our own hands, O God,
We can transform your blessing into a curse.

Almighty, I humble myself before your holy power.
From you who gave me the name of mother,
I beg aid, counsel, and insight
Into the practice and fulfillment of a mother's duties,
That they may serve in my children's
Healing and redemption, and in my own.
Grant that—unblinded by a mother's love—

I may turn a sharp eye to my children's faults,
Take those faults seriously, recognize them,
And at the right time find the best way
To address and help repair them—
To acknowledge my children's struggles
And to notice and promote my children's
Natural and enduring goodness.

Grant that I may combine love and strength
In right measure, so I might
Guide my children on the path of virtue
And raise them to be the joy of my heart,
To praise your name, and to serve humanity.
But for all those things that no human wisdom
And no human power can provide to them—please
Grant these things to them, All-Compassionate One:
Good health and strength of body and mind,
Grace and generosity of spirit,
A long life filled with good deeds,
And an abundant portion
Of life's good fortune and joy. Amen.

FOR THE MOTHER OF THE BRIDE

> *May* ADONAI *make the woman*
> *Who is coming into your house*
> *Like Rachel and like Leah,*
> *Both of whom built up the House of Israel.*

—RUTH 4:11

Eternal God, in your endless grace
You have brought me to this joyous day—
The day of my daughter's nuptial feast.
But I cannot fully indulge in my joy without placing
My hopes, wishes, and prayers before you.
How often have I, with a mother's anxious heart,
Wished for the arrival of this day on which my daughter
Might enter into the full sphere of womanhood,
To become a loving and beloved wife.
Thanks to you, O God, for preserving my life
To see this hoped-for day.

And yet it is not joy alone that moves my heart;
Fears and anxiety also seize me,
And glowing wishes and fervent prayers ascend
From the depths of my soul to your seat of mercy.

O God, grant that love, the great worker of wonders
That makes even rugged paths smooth with her charms,
That converts barren deserts into blooming fields,
Deprives the pains of life of their stings,
And changes earth into heaven—
Oh, grant that this all-conquering love
May ever dwell in my daughter's heart
And in the heart of her husband, to preserve forever
Their sweet bond of fidelity and devotion.

Grant, Almighty One, that the house
They are about to establish for themselves
May rest on the strong pillars and posts
Of your grace and mercy and on the everlasting,
Imperishable foundations of virtue and piety,
That it may ever be illuminated and surrounded
By the cheerful light of gladness and contentment,
That both may be blessed with all and in all
That brings human happiness and bliss.
Bless their marriage with good and dear children
To grow up like "blooming olive trees," adorned
With all the charms of body and soul, to be a joy
To their father and a delight to their mother. Amen.

FOR THE MOTHER OF THE GROOM

One who has found a wife has found goodness
And has brought forth favor from ADONAI.

—PROVERBS 18:22

Almighty God, you have proclaimed that
A man should leave his father and mother
And cleave to his wife,
That he should live for her and pursue by her side
The pilgrim paths of this earthly life.
Thanks to you for this day—
This solemn day on which my son shall enter
Into a sacred covenant with the wife of his heart,
With the dear being whom he has chosen
For his life's companion.
Thanks to you, above all, for preserving him,
For always surrounding him
With the wings of your grace and love,

And for saving him from life's countless dangers.
Oh, continue to be with him in all his ways
And let all his undertakings prosper.
May you, who are the source of all blessings and love,
Bless the union of love he pledges before you today
That he may find the blessing he hopes for—
A wife who will create joy for him,
A companion who will persevere with him
Through all of life's changes and opportunities.
Grant, O God, that concord and contentment
May ever dwell between them—
That even the smallest cloud not darken
The horizon of their marital happiness.

All-Gracious benefactor, One more thing
I ask of you, in whose hands our hearts rest
And who directs them as streams of water—
Grant that although my child
Shall leave his parents' house,
Filial love may never leave his heart.
Grant that his devotion to his life's companion
May not weaken or deaden his feelings
For those who gave him life and educated him—
That he may continue to be our joy and delight,
And that the love and reverence in his soul
Be preserved for a long life here on earth
And a full, divine reward in eternity. Amen.

FOR A MOTHER WHOSE
CHILD IS ABROAD

ADONAI will keep you from all evil;
God will keep your soul.

—PSALM 121:7

All-Gracious God—far from his parental home,
Far from his mother's care and concern,
My child lives in a foreign land, and I,
Who would find delight in watching over his health,
In guarding his every step,
In lavishing my undying love and faithfulness on him,
Am separated from him.
My eye, my hand, my voice cannot reach him.
I can but pray to you, my God,
For his welfare and deliverance. O Merciful One,
Hear the fervent supplication of my heart:
Take my child into your almighty protection,

Lead him safely over every rock and thorn in his path.
Endow him with such charms and grace,
With such prudent and modest deportment,
That he will win the hearts of everyone he meets.
Procure for him the friendship and benevolence
Of his neighbors, and thus turn the foreign land
Into a home for him.

Preserve the health and vigor of his body and soul,
Guard him against all evil, calamity, and danger.
Allow his soul to remain pure and clear
And cleave in childlike innocence and piety
To all that is noble and divine,
That his eye and demeanor may ever be
A brilliant mirror of his unblemished heart.
O God, grant him strength and calm,
Energy and perseverance to attend to and fulfill
All the tasks he undertakes, that they may be
A blessing and a beacon for him
And make his life happy and contented.
Help him conquer all troubles and obstacles,
And grant him all that may assist
In his present and future welfare.

O Parent of All, hear my fervent prayer
And bring my child back to me
At the right time, full of joy and the vigor of life,
To be the pride and delight of my heart,
A blessing to all, and pleasing in your sight,
My God and Sovereign. Amen.

FOR A MOTHER WHOSE SON IS IN MILITARY SERVICE

Gird your sword upon your thigh, O hero,
In your splendor and glory,
In your glory, win success.
Ride on in the cause of truth and righteous humility,
And may your right hand lead you to awesome deeds.

—PSALM 45:4–5

Almighty ruler of armies, you who reign mightily
In heaven and on earth, I raise my prayer to you
From the depths of a mother's heart.
Turn your presence toward me
And hear me in your mercy.

Following the call of duty,
My child has entered the ranks
Of those who fight on behalf of our country

To stand for what is right and proper,
To fend off threats to our nation's peace and security.
I thank you, Eternal Parent, for having given me
A child with strong, healthy limbs,
Capable of carrying out this valiant task,
But it shakes and terrifies my heart
To think of the many dangers that will surround him.
Young and inexperienced, far from the instruction
And admonitions of his parents,
How easily his heart might be tempted
To be unfaithful to his duties and to fall into sin.
Therefore I beg of you, Eternal Parent,
Take my son into your powerful protection.
Surround him with your all-encompassing grace.
Strengthen and invigorate every noble feeling
And every impulse toward good that is within him.
Strengthen and invigorate every memory
Of parental guidance and advice
That rises up in his soul—
That the teachings of virtue and fear of God
Never vanish from his sight,
That his soul not turn hard
Under the service of arms
And that no corrupting influences overcome him.

All-Compassionate One, grant my child
Insight and strength, vigor and endurance,
To fulfill his difficult duties with care and alertness
So he may be guilty of no evil or transgression
And not become confused or unstable
Amid unrelenting chaos.
And when the hot, difficult hour arrives
When he is called out to the battlefield
Where death holds its harvest—
There, Eternal Parent, surround him with your mercy.
Let your grace serve as a shield and as armor.

Steady his arm, pour courage into his heart,
And let the memory of the ancient heroes of Israel
Stir in his breast, allowing him to enter the fight
With strength and resolve.
Let my child, through his bravery and valor,
Bring honor to our people
And show faithful service to our nation.

Almighty God, hear this mother's prayer for her child!
Let my maternal blessing
Surround him like a guarding banner,
So he shall return with his service well completed,
Healthy in body and spirit,
Adorned with signs that his fulfilled duty
Has been recognized and praised—
To the joy of my heart,
To the glory and praise of your name. Amen.

FOR AN UNHAPPY WIFE

I am weary with groaning;
Every night I drench my bed,
I soak my couch with tears.

—PSALM 6:7-8

Bent down from the burden of sorrow,
I stand before you, my God,
And open my heart to you—
A heart so filled with pain—
To pour out before you my bitter regret and hurt.
Oh, the grief that presses down on me,
I dare not speak of it—except before you, my God.
My sorrow is not one that lightens when it is shared.
Rather I must and will shield it
From the eyes of the world;
Only you, All-Compassionate One,
May gaze on it and share it with me.

O God, I am married to the husband
That your eternal wisdom designated for me.
In your presence I swore holy vows
Of love and faithfulness. Yet a wedded life
In which the hearts of husband and wife
Beat for each other alone,
In which they harbor kind wishes for each other,
In which peace and love live and reign between them—
This is a good fortune
That only your chosen ones enjoy, O God.
For me, it has not come to pass.
Love does not dwell in my house,
And kindness does not live here.
Instead of mutual understanding,
All that thrives is the sullen spirit
Of conflict and argument.
Only discord and misunderstanding,
Along with their sad offspring, anger and pain,
Amble and wander through our home.

Oh, my God, what is a life without love—
Without a faithful love blessed by God
That smoothes a wife's way
And decks her path with roses,
That ushers a world
Full of blessed, holy joy into her home?
A love that is forever gentle and tender,
That covers blemishes under its cloak,
That elevates simple duties
And adorns them with crowns,
That finds its joy in sacrifice,
That, by acts of patience and loyalty,
Grows in strength and fire . . .
Where true love is lacking,
Nothing remains but artifice
And grief that consumes the heart,

Nothing but sorrow that erodes feeling
Beneath a frozen, icy breath of apathy and indifference.
How sad that I groan beneath such misfortune.
My lament rises up to you with bitter tears, my God.
Have compassion on your servant, Parent of All.

Forgive me if perhaps this grief comes about
Through my own fault—
If I have brought this sorrowful situation on myself.
Before your holy presence, I promise
To be more attentive,
To guard my feelings and thoughts,
My actions and endeavors,
And, in striving for a harmonious married life,
To remain patient and calm
So I might conquer my own heart
As well as my husband's.

O Parent in heaven, bless these intentions,
That I may find the strength and endurance
To bring them to fruition, that I not become weary
In the struggle and let my hope sink,
That I always keep my goal before my eyes,
That I stride toward it with courage,
And that my efforts yield good fortune and success.

You, Almighty One—you who guide hearts
Like channels of water—
Draw our hearts toward each other,
Let our feelings come together in love and oneness,
Let them flow into each other. You who know
The deepest strings and stirrings of our beings,
Let the stones of our hearts ring there,
Against each other.
Let our hearts unite in harmony.
Let every unholiness pass away from us

So peace might make its heavenly roof
Above our home again.
Let blessed trust and mutual care
Be a mighty shield around us,
And I shall rejoice and praise your name
Forever and ever. Amen.

FOR A WIDOW
WITH YOUNG CHILDREN

It is with you that the orphan finds mercy.

—HOSEA 14:4

I look to the poor and brokenhearted one,
Who is faithful to my word.

—ISAIAH 66:2

Let my prayer reach you, Eternal Parent,
For you dwell among
The humble and the brokenhearted,
For you inspire the courage of the deprived,
And you raise up the souls of the weak.
To you, I lift my gaze, *like a boy looking up*
To his father, like a girl gazing up at her governess.

See, O God, how I stand alone and forsaken in my life.
My husband—my protector and supporter,

The hope of my children—my husband is no more.
You have taken him from our sight,
As is your inscrutable way,
And you have called him to a better existence.
Alone now, I must raise and nourish my children.
I must be a leader and a guide for them,
A strong support, a sturdy staff. Must I be this?
Yet I, myself, need so much guidance and aid,
So much counsel and assistance.

O God, you are the parent of orphans,
The advocate of widows,
The protector of the weak and the struggling.
I call out to you from the depths of a broken heart:
Stand by me in your compassion. In my solitude,
Don't let me be consumed by worries.
Don't let me be crushed by anxieties.
Instead, let my endeavors succeed.
Bless my livelihood—
For your blessing makes the small great,
The little enough, and transforms the least action
Into a source of great redemption.
God's blessing alone makes a person rich.

Illuminate me, All-Benevolent One,
And strengthen me in the difficult work
Of raising my children,
That I might somehow compensate
For the vigilance and vigor of their father,
That I might guide my children
Down the path of virtue and holiness
And help them develop into good people
Who love the right and strive for it—
Into useful, productive members
Of their community and the larger society.
All-Compassionate One, let me find
Favor and kindness in the eyes of others,

That I may gain their true counsel and sage advice
As I embark into the world alone.
Illuminate the insight of those who offer me guidance,
And strengthen the courage of those
Who work on behalf of widows.
Let them derive generous reward in the knowledge
That they are protectors of the needy,
And grant them your holy blessing
In all that they do for me.

Almighty God, I trust and hope in you—
You who hear the plea of the humble.
My fate and future rest in your hand.
I am assured by your promise:
A parent of orphans, a champion of widows,
Is ADONAI *in the holy heights.* Amen.

FOR A MOTHER WHOSE CHILDREN PROVIDE FOR HER

Behold, I and the children ADONAI *has given me*
Are signs and symbols for Israel.

I glorify and praise you, my Sovereign and God,
You who govern me with such grace.
You have mercifully provided me
With the greatest blessings life can bring:
You have given me good and faithful children
Who surround me with their love,
Who dedicate their tender concern and hope to me.
In these days of my old age—
Days not designed for productivity or gain,
When the hands begin to tremble
And the feet no longer wish to go forward,
When rest comes often and is welcome,

My children have undertaken to provide for me.
Through their labors and energies, they are granting me
A peaceful, carefree evening to my life's days.
Oh, my God, when pious prayers for
The well-being of children
Ascend to you from the depths of every mother's heart,
How could my pleas and prayers
Not be first among them in passion and sincerity—
For the well-being of children
Who are so faithful and generous?
Oh, may the thousandfold blessing
That my grateful and loving heart showers on them
In your presence, Eternal Parent, call forth
The profound fullness of your mercy upon them.
All-Compassionate One, bless the efforts
Of my children.
Bless their labors and their occupations,
Their productivity and their endeavors.
Let all that they begin come to a successful end.
Stand by them in the struggle
Against life's adversities and conflicts.
Grant them long and happy lives,
Surrounded by your grace and your pleasure.
Keep sickness and misfortune far from them.
Grant them the complete breath and vigor
That befits such good, faithful, loving children
For whom you have granted your magnificent
Holy blessings: eternity in your presence
And a long, happy life on earth.

As for me, Eternal Parent, let me find
Mercy in your eyes
That I will never become a burden to them
Through sickness or frailty,
That I not turn into a heavy load for them
Through irritability or bad temper,

Through anger or self-pity.
Grant instead that I am able to show cheerfulness
And appreciation, that I may contribute to their lives
An advantage, an embellishment, a source of happiness;
And that through my experience and wise counsel,
I may further their success.
All-Compassionate One, please hear and grant my plea
And preserve for me the most precious good fortune
A mother can receive—the true, righteous,
Concerned love of good children. Amen.

5

PRAYERS FOR SPECIAL
CIRCUMSTANCES

FOR LIVELIHOOD

Entrust your affairs to ADONAI
And your plans will succeed.

—PROVERBS 16:3

By the sweat of your brow, you shall earn your bread.
This is your holy command, O God,
And so we must labor to acquire what we need.
Yet even when we are vigorous and work hard,
Even when we plow the furrows of our chosen field
With great diligence, energy, and effort,
Even when we stand tirelessly at the plow
And sow the seed, sometimes
You close heaven's gate to us,
Lock up the quenching dew and rain.
Sometimes you deprive us
Of the sun's vital light and warmth.
Then the sweat of our brow comes to nothing,
And all our struggling and striving is of no use.

Only your blessing, Almighty One,
Brings success to our labors.
So I pray with all my heart for your blessing,
That our plans and efforts may succeed
And that our work and toil may redeem us.
Bless our homes, that they may blossom
In fullness and prosperity.
Bless our plans and undertakings,
That our striving may bear fruit.
Grant us health and vigor of body and spirit.
Grant us renewed courage and perseverance,
Unfaltering breath in work and in love,
That we may perform our tasks
With ease and in good cheer,
And that our efforts be adequate
To support the work we do.

Let us, All-Compassionate One,
Earn our bread with integrity and righteousness,
Free from sorrow and worry,
Without reproach or shame.
Let us never lose our reliance or our trust in you—
You who *open your hand* in kindness
And sustain all living things
From your endless abundance
Of grace and mercy. Amen.

A WORKER'S PRAYER

You shall enjoy the fruits of your labors;
You shall be happy, and you shall prosper.

—PSALMS 128:2

Almighty One, you have not
Put people on earth to be idle
But rather to engage in work
And earn their bread by the sweat of their brows.
But even more than some others,
I have been called on to labor
And to toil long and hard,
For it did not please you, O God,
That I might be born to wealth and riches,
To a place in life where people breathe easy
And apply little effort at meeting their own needs.
I am poor and have no one to support me.
Everything I need I must gain with my own hands.

Yet you are indeed all-compassionate,
For you abandon none of your creatures.
You do not deny wild animals their nourishment,
The young ravens that cry out for it,
And neither will you abandon me.
You hear my cry when I call out to you.
Therefore I will never lose heart.
I will always look to you with hope
And approach my duties with cheerful courage.
All-Compassionate One, fill me once more
With a renewed readiness for work and with love.
Each morning let me wake
To a new day of good work.
Awaken within me the desire to dedicate my life
To efforts that are pleasing to you.
Lend me strength and vigor of body and spirit,
Allowing me to fulfill my tasks
Without exhaustion or fatigue.
Lend me a pious, humble bearing
And a modest heart, that I might always be
Good and reverent toward my parents
And that I might be dutiful, giving,
And faithful to those I serve
And from whose hands I earn my living.
Let me find love and esteem in their eyes.
Let me find in everyone's regard
The goodwill and respect that any person,
Even the poorest and least among us,
Can gain through holy, humble, honest conduct,
And let me find the very riches
That a person can so often lose
Through arrogance or exploitation of others.

But above all else, Eternal Parent,
Do not withdraw your love from me.
Let your blessing rest on all that I begin.

Stand by me, that I may never be
Tempted to do wrong, no matter how alluring
The opportunity may be to do so.
Guide me in the way of righteousness and innocence,
Which alone leads to honor and redemption. Amen.

IN POVERTY

ADONAI *brings death and gives life,*
God lowers to the grave and raises up.

—I SAMUEL 2:6

My God, You lead us on so many different paths in life.
Yet wherever we may wander, your love is a firm guide.
When our life's course takes us
Through smooth and blessed realms,
When it leads us through fertile, blooming fields,
Where life's lovely golden fruits are abundant,
Where the brilliance of your honor and mercy
Are virtually visible before us—my God!
And when our path leads us
Through wastelands and barren plains,
When our allotted bread is scanty and poor,
When good things elude us,
When poverty presses in on us

And only bitter effort and sweat
Yield the basic necessities of life—
Even then the spirit of your love wafts over us.
Though it may not be so visible at those times,
Childlike, pious hearts will still perceive
Your holy presence—how your banner goes with them
Through the desert night
And illuminates it. The pious heart recognizes
Every gesture of God's outstretched hand
And regards it, even when it brings suffering,
As founded in goodness—
Even when we cannot understand
What purpose such suffering could bring.

Therefore I will go calmly on my way with surrender,
Even if it is through poverty, loss, and hunger;
For you, my God, have guided me along this path.
You have apportioned the fortunes
Of rich and poor alike, for you alone know
What will truly strengthen a person
In piety and purpose, and what position and status—
Low or high, obscure or bright—
Is best suited and most fitting
To our strengths and capabilities.

If it had been up to me, I would certainly have sought
A different path. I would have chosen
A shimmering, easy path toward wealth and prosperity.
But little do I know if I would have
Traveled down it safely.
Little do I know if my heart would have gone astray
Under the influence of riches—
If it might have hardened against
The misfortunes of my neighbors,
If it might have become insensitive
To the simple, basic pleasures of life,

If it might have become dull and blinded by pride,
Given over to vanity and conceit,
Plagued by flightiness and forgetfulness of you, O God.
Meanwhile, this struggle has filled my soul
With empathy and compassion
For my fellow human beings.
It has brought me humility and patience.
It has opened my heart to the holy joy of loved ones
And the simple pleasures of their presence,
And it has taught me
To greet the smallest gift from you
As a gift of true goodwill.
It has made me value hard labor
And helped me persevere and take pride in my efforts.

In hours like these, dear God,
Let your presence and help be close at hand,
And let my hope and trust never falter.
How can I lose heart and lament?
Are you not a merciful, all-powerful God?
One word, one nod, one breath from you
And our fate changes, becoming light and bright.
You raise up the downtrodden,
Lift up the poor and unfortunate
And establish them as nobles of the land.
You send help, even when we cannot see
When or from where it might come.
Suddenly, unseen and without forewarning,
The moment of rescue and saving grace arrives
When jubilation and rejoicing infuse our hearts.
Out of seeds so full of tears,
A harvest of joy emerges.

Therefore, blessed are you, O God,
When you hold us in safekeeping,
And blessed are you, O God, when we struggle.

I will not worry or be distressed,
But *I will throw all my worries on the Holy One*,
Trusting that you love me and care for me,
And you will never deny me anything I truly need.
You will offer me all your gifts and goodness
At the appropriate time, everything that is fitting
To my ultimate well-being.

I ask only for one thing, O God:
In my poverty, let me never fall
Into the shame and disgrace
Of an immoral, hopeless life.
Rather let me, through honesty and righteousness,
Worthy activity and effort,
Gain the good wishes, love, and high regard
Of my fellow human beings. Amen.

IN PROSPERITY

Mine is the silver and mine is the gold,
Says the Ruler of Legions.

Praised be you, O God, who has created the world
And filled it with your gifts and goodness,
Bestowing benefits from the rich bounty of your grace
On all your creatures, who hope and trust in you.

Praised be you, my God,
Who has provided for me out of your plenty
And filled my house with your prosperity.
From the depths of my soul
I thank you for this, All-Compassionate One,
With my heart and mouth,
With all the strength of my being.

Yet we must come not merely with thanks that flow out
In words alone; we must also lay

An *earnest thanks offering* on the human altar.
From the blessings you have lent us, we must make
A blessing for the poor and the struggling in our midst.
With the strength we have received
From your holy generosity, we must reach out
To our less fortunate brothers and sisters
And help them strive for a better life.
With the strength you have given us,
We must seek to dry the tears of those
Who suffer and who are in need.
We must work together to undertake projects
That benefit our community,
Along with works that serve our God and faith
And uphold the honor of our people
And the well-being of our nation.
We must do these things
To the utmost of our powers and abilities.

Therefore I pray to you, Parent of All,
To lend me enough insight and knowledge
To properly put your blessings and generosity to use.
Let me never forget
That you have merely loaned them to me
So I might learn to use them wisely.
Let me never forget that one day
I will be called on to account for them.
Let me never succumb to the tendency
Of letting prosperity harden my heart against others.
May I never be so full of pride and exuberance
That I consider myself higher or better
Than my less affluent neighbors.
May I not treat my assets,
Which came to me in the midst of hardship,
With indifference or as if they had little value.
May I always remember
To honor the poor and downtrodden,
Who are also made in the image of God.

Grant, Parent of All, that I never resort to idleness
Or succumb to a pampered existence
But that I remain energetic and engaged in life
With all of its changing courses.
All-Compassionate One, lend me and my family
Good health of body and spirit,
And allow us to enjoy your blessed generosity
In happiness and joy.
Let your protection and mercy
Always surround us, and never withdraw
Your love and kindness from us. Amen.

FOR PATIENCE AND
STRENGTH IN ADVERSITY

I am the One who forms light and creates darkness,
Who makes peace and creates evil.
I am the One, maker of all these.

—ISAIAH 45:7

All-Compassionate One, my eye seeks you
Throughout the wide realms of creation.
My soul searches for you, to unburden her great woe,
To lament and pour out my sorrow.
Suffering and distress have come to me,
And my heart is full of grief.
Often, I've wanted to rage against my fate.
I've wanted to cry out against the Almighty
And ask, Have I so bitterly sinned?
Has God, the All-Compassionate One,
Turned from me in so much anger
That my tears now fall in vain
And my pleas and prayers never reach God's ear?

Misfortune weighs heavily on me,
And though I wrestle with it, I cannot conquer it.
Sadly, only in the hour of struggle
Is our own helplessness made clear.
Only in adversity do we first come to recognize
That you alone are our support and our strength—
And what boundless lessons, what infinite benefits
You have granted us through your divine law.
Torah is a strong, faithful guide for us
Throughout this earthly pilgrimage—
A mild, tireless, inexhaustible comforter
In the midst of trouble and suffering.

Like a loving mother who sits beside
Her crying infant's cradle
And sings soft, soothing lullabies,
Until finally the baby's wails give way
To a sweet little smile—
So our holy tradition rests beside
Her weeping mortal child's bed
And whispers gentle comfort into her dear one's heart
Until finally the suffering softens and disappears.
She teaches us that you are the one, Parent of All,
Who lifts all these burdens in love
And removes them—that you are the one
From whom all joy and goodness come,
That you alone are our life's good fortune and blessing.
She shows us that you deliver your tests
To precisely those you love and cherish the most,
That your love is always close to them,
That you send them strength
When they cannot go on without your help,
And that you will transform their sorrow
Into jubilation, their pain into joy.

We recall Abraham, our faithful, enlightened father,
The first to teach the world your name—

Didn't you test him severely,
Even calling him to lay down the child of his soul
As an offering on the altar?
And Jacob, the gentle, pious patriarch—
Wasn't he thrown out of his father's house
To wander into the world
With nothing but a walking stick,
Abandoned to all the dangers of life?
Yet in the midst of the desert wilderness,
You cast your protecting presence
Over his slumbering body,
And you let your angels camp nearby.
And what about David, man of my heart,
The holy singer who was captivated by God?
He, too, tasted the bitter cup of misfortune,
And the tones of deep pain resounded
Through his song-filled life.

Therefore, in my misfortune, I flee to you, my God,
And cleave to you in faith and trust.
Before you, I unburden my heart and offer my tears—
Not tears of stubbornness or defiance,
But the tears of a child in her mother's lap,
Pouring out all the sadness of her soul—
Tears that lighten the heart, wash away all bitterness,
And open my very being to hope and confidence.

In that joyful confidence, strengthened by faith in you,
I ask for your presence and your help,
That you might let my suffering end at the right time,
For you have grace and love for all your children.
Your compassion is great, and your mercy without end.
Your anger endures but a moment;
Your grace lasts a lifetime.

O God, grant only that I may never grow weary
Or weak in my resolve,

That I never allow pain and sorrow
To discourage or embitter me so
That I treat others with impatience or disrespect,
Or that I fail to be grateful
For the least gift you offer me in your grace.
May you, O God, find me worthy of your mercy
And open the gates of joy and good fortune to me,
Open the hour of rescue, the hour of deliverance,
So my eye may shed tears not of sorrow
But of joy and thanksgiving. Amen.

AFTER WITHSTANDING DANGER

ADONAI has delivered my soul from death,
My eye from tears, and my foot from stumbling.

—PSALM 116:8

In the narrow place, I called out to you, O God,
And you helped me.
Fear and trembling beat through my soul,
For danger surrounded me, and the danger was great.
Thanks to you, my God, the danger has passed me by,
And I can breathe free again.
My heart, gripped with fear, expands once more,
And, out of a calmer soul,
My prayer ascends toward you—
You who spread your grace all around me
And protected me with your almighty power
When I was encircled by danger.

God, my God, what would we be
And what would become of us
If your parental eye did not watch over us,
If your parental hand did not protect us
In danger and in need?
How great, how boundlessly exalted you are
In your goodness and your love for us.
You watch over us, you bear us
And carry us so close to your heart.

We do not always see the danger that surrounds us.
We do not always recognize the evil that pursues us.
Yet the angels of God make their camp with those
Who glorify the Holy One, to rescue them.
Even when we believe disaster has already overtaken us,
When destruction surrounds us on all sides,
When we realize that all our might and power
Are nothing—
That they will neither protect us nor save us—
Then you send your holy word,
And the danger flees from us like a vanishing shadow:
Darkness transforms into light,
And fear turns into joy and celebration.

Tears and lamentations linger at night,
But by morning, there is joy and jubilation.
Therefore, my God, I will always trust in you.
I will dedicate my heart and soul to you,
And I will never forget
That no matter how ominous or harsh the situation,
Your hand is never too short to reach us.
I will remember that you have set forth our destiny
By your unknowable wisdom and justice,
And that there is truly but one evil that faces humanity;
Namely, when we forget and lose knowledge
Of our own holy nature and your godly pleasure.

Oh, that I will never be so unfortunate
That your grace will turn away from me.

Beneath the umbrella
Of your protection, O Holy Parent,
I am protected.
Beneath your shield, I am guarded.
Help us, O God, and we shall be helped,
For you are our glory. Amen.

IN OLD AGE

Do not cast me off in old age;
When my strength fails, do not forsake me!

—PSALM 71:9

The days of our years are seventy
And, if with strength, eighty;
Their proudest success is but toil and pain,
For it is cut off swiftly and we fly away.

—PSALM 90:10

God, my God, what is life—
A dream, a shadow that passes over us,
A fleeting cloud, a sound that fades away?
Your mercy has allowed me to live
A long string of years,
But now, when I look back on them,
They seem so short and fleeting.

How entirely different my life seems now,
When I gaze back on the past,
Than when I was in the middle of it.
How entirely differently we now perceive
The emotions that governed us then—
The wishes that blazed within us,
The troubles that concerned us,
The efforts that filled us, the joys that animated us,
The good fortune we sought.
How fleeting, how vain,
How meaningless all of that seems now—
Now that it has passed and disappeared,
Now that the snow of age has cooled our passions,
Now that the perspective of long experience
Has ripened our discernment
And all of life is like a dream,
A shadow that passes over us,
A fleeting cloud, a sound that fades away.

Although looking back brings certain sorrows
Because it reveals the fleeting, emptiness of being,
Hindsight also lifts us up and brings us joy,
For through the thick clouds that obscure our past,
We can glimpse the starlight
Of your godly grace and love always shining before us—
How it elevates human understanding and insight,
How it guides and directs the course of earthly events,
Not according to the shortsighted wishes of us mortals,
But according to your eternal wisdom.
Now, for the first time, we can see
How often you have left our hopes unfulfilled
And our prayers unanswered—but only
For our own redemption and blessing;
How you have often denied us things
That we felt, with intense yearning,
Would fulfill our highest good and greatest need;

How you brought us to places in life
That we considered our greatest misfortune
And would gladly have kept far at bay;
And how, precisely through those situations,
You brought about the foundation
Of our good fortune and well-being.
Only now can we recognize this.
At times when we believed we had fallen,
We had actually been climbing upward,
And opportunities we thought would bring us
Good fortune and raise us to great heights
Would instead have led us into a pit.
No day of our lives has passed without your protection.
No hour of our lives was empty of your grace.
You have quickened our hearts with a thousand joys.
In every place, you were close to us.
In every situation, you were by our side.
In those moments when we expected it least,
Your help arrived and your gifts streamed toward us.
How can such hindsight not fill us
With the holy joy of God?
How can it not cause us to recognize,
With a deep and moving awareness,
That we have a compassionate parent in heaven,
That we are so beloved, so regarded, so cared for,
And so carried by an almighty, all-compassionate hand
That we are indeed guided and led
By one of unfathomable wisdom and goodness?

Therefore, I thank and praise you, my God,
For all that you have offered me along my life's path,
For all that was pleasant and all that was difficult—
Because you gave it all to me for my well-being.
May you forgive me if, in the course of my life,
I was overcome by what appeared to be bad fortune
Or disturbed and caught up

In the midst of what seemed to be disaster;
If I let myself doubt your love and goodness,
If I let my courage and my trust in you sink.

Grant, Eternal Parent, that I never lose
My joyful trust in you again,
That I never let my courage and faith in you falter,
Even if bodily weaknesses and the frailties of age
Should stream down upon me. Strengthen me
So that as long as I live, I am able
To fulfill my duties and obligations,
So I don't let my surroundings decline,
So I don't become argumentative or stubborn
And enter into conflict with those around me,
And so that I not trouble my loved ones
Through a long-drawn-out illness.
Grant that I be able to honor
This last portion of my life
Through good deeds toward others
And that I remain conscious and acutely aware
Of the virtues that will carry me toward you,
Into your eternal, illuminated realm. Amen.

FOR THE LEADERS
OF OUR COUNTRY

Pray for the well-being of your leader.

—PIRKE AVOT
(Ethics of the Fathers)

Almighty God, Sovereign of the entire world,
All power and might come from you.
You seat kings and regents on their thrones,
You surround them with a glint
Of your brilliant majesty,
And you bestow respect and power on them
To uphold the law and justice in the land,
To protect the oppressed and downtrodden,
To serve as a refuge for the weak and the needy,
Permitting all to flourish in safety and comfort.
We pray to you
From the depth and fullness of our hearts

For the blessing and well-being
Of the leaders of our country.

God, in your might, bless our leader
With the gifts of your love and mercy.
Grant him the finest gifts a leader can have—
His people's love, his country's peace,
And contentment in the wider realms
Affected by his office.
May he lead in good fortune and in holiness.

Bless the honored servants of our country,
The officials and advisers
Who stand at our leader's side,
So that all that passes through their hands
For the nation's benefit might thrive.
Let no turmoil rattle the gates of our land
And let no evil intentions disturb it.
Rather, let only love and trust
Come to those who govern.
Support and further their noble efforts.

May your blessing and mercy
Be with all those who serve our country,
Whether they serve with their might or their minds—
Those who uphold the law, those who spread truth,
Those who further knowledge, those who attend to art,
Those who preserve the peace, and those
Who increase our country's honor and well-being.
Send your heavenly blessing to them all,
So they might receive just reward for their efforts.
May joy and good fortune accompany their steps
And guide the work of their hands for their welfare
And for the well-being of us all. Amen.

A PRAYER FOR RAIN
IN TIME OF DROUGHT

ADONAI will open . . . the heavens for you,
To provide rain for your land in its season
And to bless all your undertakings.

—DEUTERONOMY 28:12

Almighty One, you allow your holy word
To stream across the earth, bringing forth
New shoots of every kind—
Flowers and blossoms, herbs and fruits.
And the earth, attentive to your call, opens her lap
And sends all the seeds that rest within her
Sprouting upward toward the light.

Yet see, O God, how heaven's fiery radiance
Now consumes all that the earth brings forth
And eagerly licks at the ground's juices and strength.

The earth suffers from burning thirst,
Dying for your rain,
And all of its little seedlings along with it.

So, too, we look longingly toward the mountains
And follow the course of the clouds.
But you, who set the course of all things,
Guide them past us and cause them to vanish
Without a trace. You bolt and bar
All of heaven's springs and watercourses.

Parent of All, in earnest, passionate prayer
We beg for your heavenly blessing:
O God, please do not continue to withhold
The generous deluge of your rain,
Without which all your creations will die
And fade back into the earth.
Command the clouds to let your tranquil, quenching,
Fruit-bringing rain flow down on us,
So that under this renewing and refreshing stream
The flowers will blossom forth anew,
The seeds will lift themselves up and be fulfilled,
Everything that thirsts will be refreshed,
And all that has wasted away
Will revive and return to life—
That nature, in accord with her true being,
Will once more become rich with fruits and gladness,
That she will once more be a joyful and delighted mother
To your creations, so we might turn
Our own joyous and elated gaze toward her,
And, in her blessings and riches,
See your grace and your parental love
Manifest themselves before us again.
Then, as we witness nature's wondrous beauty
And watch it blossom, we might once more perceive
The brilliance of your eternal glory and honor it. Amen.

A TRAVELER'S PRAYER

ADONAI will guard your going
And your coming
From this time forth and forever.

—PSALM 121:8

God, my Sovereign, I commend my path to you.
Wherever I wander, wherever I am,
I am under the umbrella of your protection—
Whether I am in my own secure, familiar surroundings,
Or in a strange and foreign port, I do not lose heart
And I do not fear, for I trust in you.

You who protect the tiny birds in their migration
And guide them across an unknown sea
From one hemisphere to another,
May you also take me—childlike,
With my pleading heart and longing eye—

Graciously into your merciful charge.
May your love smooth my way,
May you guard me from evil and deceit,
May you mercifully guide me to my destination,
And may you stand by me
To help me accomplish my purpose,
For the fulfillment and manifestation
Of my plans and endeavors.

Yet, All-Benevolent One, it is not for myself alone
That I lift my hands toward you.
In my fervent prayer
I also entrust to your divine care
All of my household: my loved ones
And those close to me who remain behind.
May you guard them and protect them
With your parental grace.
May you turn all harm and dire events,
All fear and danger, away from them—
So we may see one another again
In joy and good fortune. Amen.

DURING AN OCEAN VOYAGE

Those who go down to the sea in ships . . .
They have seen the works of ADONAI
And ADONAI's *wonders in the deep.*

—PSALM 107:23-24

Eternal God, Almighty Creator of the Universe,
With profound admiration and devotion
I perceive the immensity that opens up before me.
Beneath these billowing waters, in the awful deep below,
A world of beings moves,
An unfathomable number of wonders rests.
And all these beings and all these wonders
Call you, O God, their Parent and Sovereign.
They praise your name,
They rehearse your glory and majesty,
They exalt your greatness up to heaven,
Which expands over these waters

With its myriad stars and worlds,
Whose brilliant, luminous forms
Are reflected a thousandfold
In the smooth surface of the ocean.

My God, how small I feel,
How insignificant in this immense creation.
Full of fear and humility, I ask myself,
What am I in this boundless universe
Among this endless number of worlds and creatures?
What are human beings that you are mindful of them,
Mere mortals, that you look down on them?
And yet you have exalted us above all other beings.
You have crowned humanity with glory and honor,
Given us dominion over the works of your hand,
And put all things under our feet.
Yes, you have put us in charge
Of the whole of creation,
Allowed us to command even the ocean
With its mighty monsters,
Let us turn its floods into a path
To carry us and our possessions.

All human power rests in your grace, O God,
And in your infinite love.
You carry and support us,
Whether we pass over valley and mountain
Or over the sea's rolling waves.
Your light illumines us, your power strengthens us,
Belief in you affords us the wisdom and courage
To conquer dangers and troubles, waves and winds.
But at a nod of your head
The earth heaves and trembles,
And with it we mortals.
The heights and depths rise,
And we and our power are gone.

Oh, may your mercy never forsake me
During this perilous voyage.
As you safely carried Noah's ark
Through the mighty waters of the flood,
So may you guide this vessel
That carries me and my companions.
Surround it with your almighty protection
That it may be borne on the wings
Of soft and favorable breezes,
And lead us safely and unharmed
To the place where we are bound. Amen.

DURING A STORM AT SEA

Who makes the winds God's messengers . . .

—PSALM 104:4

God, my refuge and my protection—
Fear shudders through me.
Fog and wind surround us in the water's depths,
And the sea's wild waves stream higher.
This weak, tottering house of planks
Is like a ball tossed back and forth
By the tumultuous waves.
But take courage, my heart; do not falter.
Amid the dangers and terrors that bear down on me
I am not alone. God—the All-Powerful,
The All-Compassionate—is by my side.
Over the storming waves and flood,
God's spirit hovers and rests.
Over the waves of this wild, roaring ocean,

The voice of the Eternal One resounds:
The voice of God goes forth over the waters,
The voice of God over the mighty waters.
To you, Almighty One,
You who command the raging flood,
You who command the wild whirling of the storm,
To you I flee. To you I pray
From the depths of my fear-struck soul:
Help us, Holy Parent, and stand by us.
Do not give us over to destruction.
Let us not become fodder for the abyss
That reaches out to swallow us.
Spread the presence of your eternal might
Around our bodies,
And guide us with the fullness of your mercy
Away from these awesome and unholy depths
To a safe port, to a harbor of refuge
Back on dry land once more—
And I will thank you all the days of my life.

THANKSGIVING FOR
A SAFE JOURNEY

For the sea is God's, and God has made it,
And God's hands have fashioned the dry land.

—PSALM 95:5

Praise and thanks to you, my God and protector.
Again I stand on dry land, again
The kindly earth is spread out beneath my feet
In all its joyful beauty.
From the depths of my soul
I thank you, All-Good God.
Thank you for graciously protecting me
On a dangerous voyage when nothing
But a weak, shaky plank separated me
From the abyss in whose awful depths
Death and destruction are constantly lurking.
You, O God, are the ruler of worlds.

Your spirit hovers over the waters,
Your grace was with me. You carried me safely
Over rocks and through tempests,
Through waves and raving billows.
You bound back the wings of the storm
Before whose unbridled rage
The depths of the sea tremble
And we mortals, with all our skill and wisdom,
Stand powerless.

Oh, may you continue to be with me
And guide me safely
Over all the rocks and billows of life.
May you guard and protect me against all mishaps.
May you deliver me from all malicious assaults
And every persecution that may rage around me,
As well as from destructive storms of emotion
Whenever they should arise within me.

Great, O God, are the dangers and temptations of life.
Within and around us are shadowy realms
That could harm or destroy us, but with your help
We can conquer and withstand all of these.
Yours is the power and the strength.
Unto you belong all glory, praise, and majesty
From eternity even to eternity. Amen.

6

PRAYERS FOR HEALING

WHEN A HUSBAND IS ILL

ADONAI will fortify a person on his sickbed.

—PSALM 41:4

Almighty One, I take refuge in you—
You who have always been my rescue and my help,
I seek comfort and deliverance.
My husband, the father of my children,
The crown of my life,
Has been stricken with pain and sickness.
I see his life threatened;
And with fear and trembling, I ask,
From where does my help come?
I don't expect my help to come from any mortal.
Human help is weak and faltering;
It splinters like a matchstick
Against your almighty will.
Human insight is blind when no beam of light

Comes from above to enlighten it.
Power and strength lie in your hands alone.
Only you are a true healer,
Faithful and full of compassion.
Therefore, Eternal One, I await your help.
My eyes look to you in longing and in hope.
My praying lips speak to you.
My heart calls out to you in silent pain,
And my entire being dissolves before you
In fervent wish and prayer.

O All-Compassionate One, hear me
And let me feel your presence.
Save my husband for me!
Grant him full health once more.
Give him strength for his family,
For his occupation, for his duties
And his daily activities. Preserve him
For the sake of our poor, innocent children,
As their provider, as the one who raises them,
As their "protector on earth,"
As you have assigned him to be.
Preserve my devoted companion in life, O God,
Keep my faithful beloved on this earth!
He is the sun, the light of my days;
If the sun is gone,
Then darkness and night will be my lot.
He is the pillar of my house;
If it falters, then everything I have
Will sink, tremble, and collapse.
At his side I go my way undaunted
Along paths beset with problems;
With strength and courage I carry
Everything that you, O God, present to me.
But without him I'm a tendril without support,
A mastless and rudderless ship
On the open, stormy sea.

God, be merciful to me.
Do not be mindful of my sins and failures.
Do not punish me in your anger,
Do not chastise me in your wrath.
Remember me in your boundless compassion,
And accept my pious intentions
Kindly and with forgiveness
Accept my promise to do better,
My earnest apologies, my sincere efforts
To stand beside the misfortunate and needy
With love and kindness,
To travel the path of right and devotion,
To flee from sinful impulses.
May you accept these deeds as a pleasing offering,
And may they bring to me and my husband
Your mercy and your compassion.
O Eternal One, please send me your compassion.
With your help, Parent of All, grant me pardon.

You, O God, benefactor, friend,
And helper of all your children—
You count every tear our eyes shed,
You are near to all whose hearts are broken,
You stand lovingly and compassionately
Beside the bodies of the sick.
O Eternal Parent, also stand
Beside me and my husband.
Let the awareness of your closeness
Be a sweet, healing comfort in my sorrow;
For I am not alone, not forsaken in my grief.
You, Eternal Parent, stand as witness to my tears.
You see my pain. You look down on my suffering,
And you, source of all compassion and all mercy,
Will also grant me your compassion.
You will let your merciful sun rise for me,
And you will not deny me your help.
May I not be put to shame in my hope and trust.

May your love never stray from me.
May your heavenly comfort lift my heart,
And may you be my merciful guide
Through the troubles that oppress me.
Let my sorrow turn into joy, O God,
For you are my support and my hope. Amen.

WHEN A FATHER IS ILL

You shall serve ADONAI, *your God,*
And ADONAI *will bless your bread and your water*
And will remove illness from your midst.

—EXODUS 23:25

My prayer, poured forth this day before you,
All-Merciful Parent, is more in tears than in words—
In tears abundant and burning,
Produced by anguish and anxiety.
For what is more saddening for a child's heart
Than to know that her dear father is lying
On a bed of suffering and sickness?
I trust and hope in your mercy, yet still
I tremble with fright as I bow before you
To beg you for the life and health
Of my beloved father. As you have proclaimed,
"You shall seek my face!"

And I seek your face with a longing heart.
Oh, don't hide it from me.
Hear my fervent prayer!
Don't let my tears flow in vain before you.
Have mercy upon my dear father.
Quicken him with the soft dew of your grace,
Mercifully pour your healing balm on his wounds,
And let the rays of your goodness and compassion
Descend on him, that he might be
Uplifted by their warmth
And restored to strength and vigor.
Forgive him, O All-Good Parent, of any errors
He may have committed, and remember
All the good and charitable deeds he has performed.
Oh, let these deeds intercede for him now
Before your throne of justice and mercy.

May my fervent prayer come before you
That the hour of deliverance and redemption
May soon arrive and our tears of woe
Be transformed into tears of joy and gratitude. Amen.

WHEN A MOTHER IS ILL

O God, please heal her!

—NUMBERS 12:13

All-Merciful One, see me here before you,
Lost in deep, bitter pain,
Languishing in fear and suffering,
My mother, my beloved mother, is ill.
Every cry, every sound of suffering from her lips,
Every sigh runs through me with nameless pain.
For she, the faithful, loving one
Who has done and endured so much for me,
Is in need of great, all-powerful help.
And I—what can I, in my powerlessness,
Do on her behalf? I can do nothing—
Nothing except throw myself before you, O God,
Raise my hands in entreaty before you,
And with hot, burning tears cry out for your mercy.

O Parent of All, send us
Your saving, all-encompassing help.
Preserve my beloved mother, my friend and counselor.
Grant her the strength to withstand her suffering.
Grant her new health and energy for life.
Be mindful of all her diligence,
All her faithfulness and love,
Which always filled her maternal heart,
And let her partake of your faithfulness and love.
You are the sovereign and ruler of life and death.
A word, a glance from you
Can transform our house of suffering
Into a house of joy,
Our lamentation and cries of pain
Into jubilation and thanks.
All-Compassionate One, you take pleasure
In bringing joy to all of your creations—
Let your blessed word be said.
Let your healing, life-giving gaze rest on us.
Tell us that my mother will live,
That she will be healthy!
With jubilation and thanks I will praise you
And dedicate my entire life to you in pious love. Amen.

WHEN A CHILD IS ILL

Please, ADONAI, save us now!

—PSALM 118:25

Almighty God, pain and suffering clutch at my heart.
Gripped with sorrow, I lift up my hands
To implore you! You alone, my Creator—
You who have forged the human heart
And hear its melancholy music—
You alone know the feelings that move a mother.
You alone know the multitude of sufferings
That surround a mother's fear:
My child is ill, my child is in danger.

Before the throne of your mercy,
I take refuge at this time of need.
All-Compassionate One, I take shelter
Beneath your shield

From the force of my grief and fear.
O Almighty God, accept my prayer with mercy.
Let me witness your love and your compassion.
Give my soul no cause for fear
And my heart no cause for sorrow.
Preserve my child for me!
Let my child be whole and healed.
Bound by a thousand threads, my soul hangs
At my child's side.
This tender being is my blood, my flesh, my life.
With love and pain, I bore this little one and raised it.
I cared for my offspring and nourished it;
With anxiety and love, I have watched
Every hour of my child's life.
In fervent fear and love, my tears flow today.
My heart cries out to you: *Hear me!*
Be merciful, Eternal Parent. *Be merciful!*
Grace me with a healthy child once more—
This tender flower, barely touched
By the light of day—
Let me once again see my child's delighted laughter,
Let me once more see my child's cheerful play,
And I will thank you all the days of my life.
I will marshal all my strength to raise my child
In a way that pleases you, so my babe's life
Will be dedicated to you, with your holy name
Forever engraved on [this] young heart
So my child will learn to honor you
And pray to you throughout life.
Eternal Parent, do not cast me away.
Do not punish me for my sins;
Do not chastise me in your wrath.
In your mercy, forgive my *guilt*
For the sake of my child's *innocence.*
Preserve my child's beautiful life for me,
This precious jewel that has so illuminated

And hallowed my heart and my home,
Filling it with pure and holy joy.
All-Benevolent One, hear my passionate, fervent plea.
All-Compassionate One, send me your help,
For I hope and trust in you. Amen.

WHEN AN ADULT CHILD IS ILL

He shall not break even a bruised reed
Nor snuff out even a dim wick,
But he shall bring forth the true way.

—ISAIAH 42:3

Heavy anguish weighs on my heart, O God.
My beloved, precious child, whom I raised to adulthood
With pain and joy, with effort and care—
My child lies ill, with [his/her] strength broken
And [his/her] precious body surrounded by danger.

Sustain for me, O Compassionate One,
The cherished gift you gave me.
Return the child with whom you blessed me
And who is more to me than all earthly treasures.
Turn misfortune away from my child,
Protect my dear one from harm.

Don't let this affliction
Take possession of my child's being,
Don't let it arrest my offspring in the blossom of life
And cut off my child's years before they are completed.

Witness my fear, dear God, how my knees falter,
How my heart breaks from pain and sorrow.
I cannot express my cry through prayers and words,
For a mother's pain has no words;
A mother's grief has only tears—
And hot, burning tears are streaming from my eyes.
Oh, that they may find their way to you
And that you allow them to descend as cooling dew,
As a healing balm on my child's body.

O my God, since you consider a mother's
Pious words of blessing pleasing enough
To bring well-being to her child throughout life,
Won't you also answer a mother's fervent plea
And bring your help, your saving grace,
And your mercy to her child?
All-Merciful One, you are my staff and my support.
I rest my hope in your compassion
And your boundless goodness.
If my child or I have brought this misfortune
On ourselves through any failing or misdeed,
Please treat us with mercy.
Send us your forgiving grace,
And let my child's affliction and my pain
Be our atonement.
Grant us your pardon and your healing. Amen.

A PRAYER FOR HEALING

You crush a person to dust,
And say, "Return, O mortal child!"

—PSALM 90:3

From my painful resting place,
I lift my eyes to you, O God,
My God—you who injure
And then bind up injuries,
You who wound and then heal again,
You have brought a serious illness upon me.
My limbs are weak,
And a fiery fever sears through my body.
Yet in the midst of my suffering and pain,
You, O God, are my hope and my trust.
You are my staff and my support.
Though my flesh and my heart may fail,
God is the rock of my heart and my portion forever.

I do not rely on human help,
For human understanding and wisdom
Wander in darkness and so easily go wrong.
When you don't illuminate us with your light,
When you don't set us on the path of redemption,
When you don't choose us to be
A tool for your mercy or a servant of your healing,
Then all care and efforts are useless and for nothing.
Yet one nod from you alone,
The source and wellspring of all life, is enough
To return my lost strength to me once more
And guide me back again
To the warm, blossoming richness of life
To which I am attached
By a thousand precious, holy threads.

So may you let it be, my God, through your mercy.
Let me once more be healthy and vibrant
In life and in soul.
Let me return once again
To my work and my daily activities,
To the beloved circle of my friends and family,
To the useful labor and faithful life
Of my fellow human beings. Amen.

DURING A LONG ILLNESS

Only I, ADONAI, *have been your God*
Ever since the land of Egypt;
You have never known a true God but me;
You have never had a helper other than me.

—HOSEA 13:4

My God and Creator, bowed down and broken
From my long suffering, I appear before you
To seek your protection, your strength, and your help.
O, this condition robs my heart of all spirit and joy
And allows bitter, painful feelings to arise within me.
My body's frailty can be
A sorry influence on my soul.
Often I become irritable or easily excited;
Often I become frustrated with my environment,
Impatient with what you have sent me
And what you have decreed.

At these moments I forget how all that comes to us,
Even the painful and difficult,
Flows from your eternal compassion and wisdom
And is intended only for our redemption.

O God, you in your boundless parental grace
Would certainly not let me suffer for no use.
Either you send me this suffering
As a result of my many sins and failings,
As a means for my improvement,
As a warning and reminder
To return to the holy and right,
And as a means of turning my heart
Away from emptiness and vanity,
Making me more sensitive and humble;
Or else you send me this suffering as a trial,
As a measure of my faith and trust in you,
To give me the opportunity to test myself,
To discover the depth of my feelings
And the wellspring of my inner strength.

If it is a result of my wrongdoing,
Then shouldn't I carry it in humility,
In childlike patience and submission,
With the hope that I might encounter through it
The intent of your holy wisdom?
And if it is a trial, then shouldn't I gather
All the strength of my soul,
All the courage, all the vigor of my heart,
To come before you, my God, on whom I rely,
To endure this test you have given me
With firm resolve and without fail?

Oh my God, stand by me,
That my heart may be strengthened,
That it may shine with confidence and trust,

That it may bear calmly, in a heightened state,
The pain and suffering this condition brings.
My heart yearns toward you,
Awaiting your grace and hoping for your mercy.

Your mercy, O God, is my comfort and my hope.
Why should I falter, why should I succumb
To misery and despair?
Your parental grace and love embrace all your children;
So, too, do you hold me within your loving heart.
After a night of dense fog, you send
A shower of invigorating sunshine to the earth;
So, too, will you send into my life,
Which has been a long, gloomy night,
The brilliant, joyous beam of renewed energy.
After every winter, you bring forth
The gentle breath of spring
To give new life to the frozen ground;
So too will you enliven my sapped strength
With the fresh breeze of well-being, bringing me
To renewed life, renewed works, and renewed labor
In the circle of my loved ones and friends.

Oh, so may you let it be for me.
May the reviving dew of your grace
Soon shower down on me,
Bringing me your mercy, saving me,
And uplifting me with your love. Amen.

AT A PLACE OF HEALING WATERS

You can draw water with joy
From the springs of salvation.

—ISAIAH 12:3

I

Great are your works, O God.
The whole earth is filled with your goodness.
You have created a soothing balm for every hurt,
A healing herb for every wound.
Soon we will find blessing in a bubbling spring
That shoots forth from hard rock.
Soon we will discover it in a field of blossoming flowers.
It will bloom for us on the mountain's heights,
And soon it will be released from the earth's deep wells.
Yet our human perspective can be so narrow,
Our perception so weak, that often we seek things

That have no purpose and do us no good.
The earth blooms at our feet, and we fail to see it.
The earth turns green all around us,
And we know nothing of it.

O God, here may I find the balm for my wounds.
May your goodness be witnessed through me,
So good health—such a precious treasure—
May be mine.
May I return home to my loved ones free of suffering,
With a joyous heart and an elevated soul,
That I might use all my strength
For the joy and benefit of those around me,
For the blessing of my fellow human beings,
And to your glory and perfection,
My God and Sovereign. Amen.

II

Almighty God, I have so much
To implore of your heavenly mercy,
Yet one desire is most urgent on my lips,
One supplication that rises up before all others—
An impassioned plea for the return and renewal
Of my good health.
I have left my home and household,
The circle of my loved ones,
My husband, my children, and my daily activities,
To seek healing and recovery for my physical ailments
In the bosom of your miraculous natural world.
Oh, don't let my hope be in vain!
Don't let me knock at the door to your mercy
For nothing.
Send me an angel of recovery—as it is written,
When we call on God, God hears us
And sends word that we will recover—

So I might once again experience
The blessed feeling of good health,
That long-desired sense of well-being;
So I may once again take joy in perceiving
Your wondrous creation with a full, untroubled soul,
So I might return to my life and occupation
With renewed energy and enjoyment,
With newfound strength and cheerful confidence.

Sustain me, dear God, and guide me
To live in a way that supports and fosters
My good health. Stand by me
And strengthen me with sufficient resolve
To avoid all that would thwart my recovery—
So that no harmful habit or desire,
No tempting pursuit or practice,
Might disturb my health again.
Heal us, God, and we shall be healed.
Help us, and we shall be helped.
For you are our glory, our hope,
And our support forever. Amen.

THANKSGIVING FOR RECOVERY

> **ADONAI** *punished me severely*
> *But did not hand me over to death.*
>
> —PSALM 118:18

Eternal Sovereign, full of mercy, how I thank you
For the healing you have allowed me to receive.
Seriously ill, tortured by pain and suffering,
I was laid flat, drained of strength,
Surrounded by fears of death.
But in the narrow place,
I called out to you, and you helped me!
From death's murky alleyways
You have guided me back
Into life's gleaming meadow.
Instead of the shadow of death
You have given me the cheerful light of day.
You have not separated me from my friends

And all those who are so beloved and dear to my heart.
In your mercy, you have given us back to one another
And reunited us. With such delight,
I feel myself growing stronger each day.
I feel health streaming through me.
Praise and thanks to you, Most High.
Every new heartbeat is a prayer
Of thanks and praise to you.
Every hour of my existence
Is dedicated to you in love and gratitude.

All-Compassionate One, you have given me life
For the second time,
Even though I don't greet it now
As I did the first time,
With a child's innocence and purity.
Yet I hope that through my suffering
I have been able to atone for some things.
I hope I have been purified and cleansed,
So I might begin my life anew.

How precious life is!
Until this moment I have often spent my days
Frivolously, without much use or piety.
I often frittered my time away
In idleness or worthless diversions,
Occupying myself with activities
That are total strangers to life's true purpose.
From now on I resolve
To pay better attention to my time.
No day shall be lost to me.
Each day shall be of value for my work on this earth,
For my soul's redemption, for my heart's fullness—
And every night I will ask my inner judge
To assess my day's work.
From now on I will open my heart

To every joyful influence.
I will celebrate the good
That the Holy One provides for me,
Even when that good is but a small one.
I will rejoice in the good fortune of my neighbors,
And I will be happy for whatever chance I may have
To do something useful for them.

I will struggle with strength and endurance
Against everything that is hard and unholy in my life.
With courage and with patience,
I will strive to lighten and improve it.
And when my struggle feels hopeless,
I will bring my concerns and worries
To the Parent of All, the One who cares for me,
The One who helps me carry heavy burdens,
The One who supports me when I falter,
The One who gives me confidence
And grants me redemption.
To the Holy One, I entrust my way,
And God guides me in safety.
When all forsake me, when no one can or will assist me,
Then you, O God, are my never-tiring help and rescue.
I hope for your eternal help. Amen.

AT THE END OF LIFE

My God, the days that shall be mine
Are set forth in your book
As if none of them had yet occurred.
And should you decide to call me
From this life so soon,
Oh, I beg of you, Eternal Parent,
Teach me to surrender to your holy will
And to honor your decision with humility,
So I might leave this world in peace
And with great courage.
For this life is so often a bitter school of tests,
Designed to prepare and develop our souls
For the elevated realm of the world to come.

Eternal Parent, fortify me and lift my spirits
In the comforting knowledge
That death is but a devoted messenger
Of your great majesty and profound compassion;
For death guides the painful, failing body
Into a peaceful, eternal sleep—while the soul,

Limitless in free and glorious strength,
Ascends to her godly home,
Where her highest joys await
In the circle of enlightened friends
Who have gone before us.

Those beloved and precious ones
Whom I leave behind me here,
I entrust to your eternal love and mercy.
Continue to be a protection and a shield for them,
A parent and a friend,
A guide and a leader on all of their paths.
Usher them gently and tenderly through life
On a course of virtue and righteousness,
Toward eternity, where I will be awaiting them.

All-Compassionate One, may you forgive all my sins.
May you take me up beside you in your mercy
So my soul may go to her rest
Purified, cleansed, and forgiven. Amen.

7

MEMORIAL PRAYERS

ON THE ANNIVERSARY
OF A PARENT'S DEATH
יאָר־צייט

Little burning lamp, so gentle and pure,
My mother's life was as bright
And cheerful as your shining light.
Without rest, she strove upward,
But, alas, she also faltered
Like the flicker of your flame.

—ATTRIBUTED TO LIPPMANN MOSES BÜSCHENTHAL
(German, d. 1818)

Though my thoughts of you,
Holy spirit of my beloved [father/mother],
So often occupy my heart, they do so
Even more powerfully today, on the anniversary
Of your separation from this life.
My whole being stirs with deep melancholy.

This day takes me back to the days
When you were still alive, when your love
Guided me with such tenderness and care,
When I drew comfort from your presence in hard times
And when you reveled in my joys.
I envision you before me now,
Your face shining with love, your tender gaze.
Your voice echoes through my soul
As if it had only just faded away.

God has called you away from here,
And nothing is left to me from your beloved being
Except your precious memory
And the wise teachings and insights
That you conveyed to me during your lifetime.
Pious and childlike, I will hold on to these.
I will treasure them as your most precious legacy.
I will observe them and preserve them
That they may never be lost to me.
My memories of you along with my own life's course
Are a precious bond between us.
Every good deed I do, guided by your memory,
Serves as a bond of love
And springs from my devoted wish and will
To please and honor you,
Even in the world beyond.

And you, All-Benevolent One,
You who are Parent and Sovereign of All
In the heavens above and on the earth below,
May this child's mourning be acceptable to you,
So you might heed my prayer
To take up the purified soul of my [mother/father]
Mercifully into the realm of your brilliance,
Into the circle of your holy angels,
That the soul of my dear parent(s) may take part

In every blessedness beyond knowing—
Blessedness we cannot now perceive
But for which we truly yearn.

As for me, my God, stand by my side
With your love, your counsel, and your help.
Place your holy comfort into my heart
And teach me throughout my entire life
To be in awe of God and virtue,
That I may always be worthy
Of the pleasure and love of those precious ones who
    dwell so close to you.
Amen.

AT A FATHER'S GRAVE

All-Merciful God, in this silent field,
Where the earthly remains of my departed father rest,
I dedicate my tears and emotions to his memory.
Now that I have lost my dear father
From this earthly life
I fully know what a treasure of love
I once possessed in him.
He—the faithful guide of my youth,
My monitor and counselor—wisely watched over
The ennoblement of my spirit
And strengthening of my body.
He enlightened my mind and filled my heart with love.
He submitted joyfully to all the struggles of life
So I might gain the joys of life. O my dear father,
Remembering you, my tears stream forth
And my heart overflows with love and grief.
But what good can my love do for you now?
It can no longer cause you earthly joy and happiness—
You, who are far removed
From all earthly wishes, wants, and cares.

But doing good, practicing charity,
Ennobling the heart—
These are the heavenly joys
A child may prepare for a blessed father.
And these joys I will prepare for you
By performing good actions
In your name and in your spirit.
These shall be the sacrifices I will offer up
On the altar of my love.
May God record them in the Book of Eternal Life
For your blessing and redemption
In your heavenly home.

O God of heaven and earth,
As my righteous father has left behind,
In paternal love, his blessings for me,
So do I, from a child's love,
Bless his memory before you
And pray to you for the redemption of his soul.
Oh, may you remember him in love and mercy.
May you remember every noble deed,
Every good action he performed on this earth,
And graciously forgive whatever sin and transgression
He may have committed out of human weakness.
And may all the sufferings, troubles, tribulations,
And hardships he endured during his earthly journey
Be his atonement and sacrifice before you,
That he might partake of eternal peace, blessing,
And redemption in your divine presence. Amen.

AT A MOTHER'S GRAVE

Here by this silent mound
Where you, beloved Mother, sleep in death's lap—
A sleep that robbed me
Of my heart's most loyal friend,
The one who raised and cared for me—
Here I pray to God for your redemption.
Here I recall your image,
Your gentle, loving presence on this earth,
That they may never be extinguished from my heart.
Here I pledge to always live true to your teaching
And your motherly advice
To always pursue the path of virtue.

I well know that beneath this mound
Lie only dust and ash,
And that your true and actual being
Has been drawn upward as pure spirit
To the hallowed regions of the angels,
And that your motherly gaze
Rests on me wherever I may be.

Yet when I tread on this ground
And approach this place,
I feel as if I come closer to you,
That when I clutch this earth that covers you,
I hold a part of you;
And when I let my tears flow here,
I weep against your faithful heart.

My God, on this ground so sacred to me,
I offer up my prayer to you
To rest the soul of my faithful mother.
Take her—she, whose heart always beat
With the warmth of a mother's love—
Joyfully into your higher realm of love.
She, who in her motherly tenderness
Never counted the sacrifices she made,
Never weighed the care she gave,
Never measured the suffering she gladly accepted
For the sake of her child's well-being—
For her, may you also not count and not weigh
Any sins she committed before you
Or anything lacking from her life as a mortal being.
Just as she poured out joys and blessings
On her child here below, so surround her soul above
With a paradise of the same.

As for me, Eternal One,
May my mother's constant love,
Which always filled her soul,
Be enough to bring her the blessing
She asked of you so often—
A blessing for her child of your mercy and compassion,
That your love and godly strength
Might always remain by my side,
That you might guide me with a gentle hand
Through this earthly valley,

And that my soul may one day
Go to its rest and reunion
With those beloved ones
Who have gone before me. Amen.

AT A HUSBAND'S GRAVE

Hannah answered and said,
"No, my lord, I am a woman of aggrieved spirit.
I have drunk neither wine nor strong drink,
And I have poured out my soul before ADONAI."

—I SAMUEL 1:15

I am drawn here, to death's silent dwelling place,
As sad and dreary as it is—for here,
Surrounded by the dark night of the grave,
My beloved husband rests.
Here my burning tears may flow onto his tomb
And my keening may be heard by no one.
Far from life's tumult, no stranger's eye,
No unsympathetic word, violate my grief.
You alone, O my God, are witness to the pain
That resides in the depths of my soul.
The world that once held so much beauty

Now is dark, and all its joys are draped
In a black veil of mourning.

May you, O Parent of All, not be angry with me
That I grieve so bitterly, that my soul mourns
So deeply over what you have ordained.
My God, I do not presume to murmur against
Your verdicts and censure your ways;
You are the God of love and wisdom.
What mortal could possibly
Perceive and understand you?
Who could presume to judge your ways
And ask you, What do you do?
Whatever you do is well done;
Therefore, I adore you in the dust
And humbly pay homage to your inscrutable counsel.
But can I command my heart not to feel my misfortune?
Can I say to my grief, Flee from me!
Or to my mourning soul, Be cheerful?

And why shouldn't my soul mourn
Now that its soul mate has been torn from it?
Why shouldn't my eyes be filled with tears
Now that the most brilliant star of my days
Is extinguished, now that
The prop and pillar of my house
Is broken, the blossom and adornment of my life
Withered, and the most precious treasure of my heart
Given up to decay?

But no! Only his earthly part,
His body, his tenement of dust
Has been returned to dust from where it came,
But his nobler being, his immortal part, his spirit,
Continues to live with all its thoughts and feelings,
With all its faithfulness and love.

Dust returns to the earth as it was,
And the spirit ascends to God, who gave it.
Thus it is written in your holy book.
I shall always cling to this hope and promise;
The thought that death cannot have completely
Destroyed the bond of our hearts
Shall be my comfort in my mourning,
Balm to my wounded soul.
As my love follows him into the next world,
So will he—and I am convinced of this—
Look down with his love and his blessing
On me and our children, whom he has left behind.
As I raise my tearful eye in fervent prayer
To you, my God, to implore heavenly redemption
On *him*, he will in return invoke your mercy
And grace on *us*, and thus our souls will meet
On the steps of your throne.

But to you, O All-Good Parent in heaven,
You who watch over orphans and widows
From your sacred heights, to you I confide my life,
Now deprived of its earthly protection,
And now that my children are bereaved
Of their guide and supporter.
May your love surround me,
Your almighty power strengthen me,
Your wisdom enlighten me,
That I may walk through life with strength and courage,
That I may fulfill the duties and obligations
That are now my lot in double measure
With a brave spirit and a gentle heart,
To govern my house with understanding and endurance
And to be able to meet all its needs. Amen.

AT A CHILD'S GRAVE

I say, "Leave me alone;
I will weep bitterly.
Do not insist on comforting me
For the calamity of my people."

—ISAIAH 22:4

God, you are all-powerful in your might,
Terrible in your justice!
You stretch out your hand
And the sun's blaze is extinguished.
You speak, and the earth shudders.
Your breath blows, and huge cedars crash.
Green fields, freshly sprouted and newly blossoming,
Turn into barren, harsh wastelands.
As for a human being full of vivacious youth,
Full of untried hopes that enrich a fortunate life—
You send out your solemn emissary of death.

See how the blossom wilts,
How it withers and topples into dust.

Beneath this mound rests the flower of my heart,
My flesh and blood, the center of my life, my child.
It would be in vain now if I dissolved into pain,
If tears streamed from my eyes.
You, O God—you who created and designed
The innermost depths of the human heart—
You know more than anyone
What a child is to a mother,
How a mother's heart is tied to her child
With all the threads and fibers of her being,
How they are intertwined with each other.
And when death places its cold hand on the child,
When death tears a child from a mother's side,
Then her entire heart is wrenched
Into a bleeding wound.

So do not be angry at my pain, O God.
Have mercy on me in my suffering.
Pour your holy comfort into my heart.
Give me the strength to bear this
And to resign myself to it.

Surely everything you do is for a reason.
Your eternal wisdom, its mysterious ways—
How could a human being's limited vision
Ever grasp its foundations?
Your ways are dark and incomprehensible,
Yet whatever you do is for our redemption.
You are our parent and we are your children,
You are our king and we are your people,
You are our shepherd and we are your flock.
How would you determine anything for us
Except for our own redemption?

So let me, O God, find comfort
In your love and faithfulness.
Let my entire being be permeated
With the words of your exalted teaching
And the words of our hallowed tradition.
Strengthen my faith so I can trust
That you have taken up my unblemished child
With love and kindness into your heavenly embrace,
And that you have removed my child's pure soul
To shelter it from the pain and suffering
Of this world.

All-Benevolent One, let my child
Look down on me like a shining angel.
Let my child's perfect image always remain before me.
Let my angel's voice warm me
When I am in danger of failing you.
Let my child's gaze rest on me
When I have done something worthy of merit,
And eventually let me be reunited with my child
When you call me into your heavenly realm. Amen.

AT A RELATIVE'S GRAVE

A human being is like a breath;
A person's days are like a passing shadow.

—PSALM 144:4

Dear one, you meant so much to me,
And now you are separated from me,
You were loving to me during your lifetime,
And now I come to your resting place
To express my feelings and my love
To your enlightened soul in the world beyond
And to pray here to God for your eternal peace.
May the All-Benevolent One hear my sincere wishes:
May your body find a gentle rest here,
And may your spirit be hallowed
And filled with joy in heaven.

We should come to this place often
To be fully aware of how empty this world truly is,

262 * HOURS OF DEVOTION

To become fully conscious
Of our higher calling on earth.
What is our whole earthly life?
One span of time and we stand at the grave.
Our life's path, whether crowned
With blossoms of joy and contentment
When good fortune walks hand in hand with us,
Or as bleak as a flowerless trail of stones,
Darkened by misfortune, made barren by thirst—
Where else does this path lead except to these gates?

And these gates open for us,
Whether we stand in youthful beauty
Or are stooped over by old age.
Death takes us all, and we all turn to ash.
Everything we did in darkness like sleepwalkers
Sinks in ruin and collapse. Yet only the shell caves in.
The actual being remains unchanged.
The mortal husk breaks apart, but the spirit rises up
To its eternal residence in the world to come.
How good it is for us if we are true to our convictions,
If we bring our journey on this earth to full completion,
If in all the struggles and worries of life
We never allow our eternal purpose
To disappear from consciousness,
If we go into infinite splendor
Purified and enlightened,
Accompanied by works of love and justice.

Oh, my heart—learn here
To make something worthy of your life.
Learn to make use of your days of good fortune—
Just as your days of misfortune serve
To redeem and develop your undying spirit—
So in the last days of my life
May I look back without regret or remorse

So my soul can go in peace and holiness
To dwell with my ancestors.
May this be your will, O Holy One, my God.
Grant me your blessing and your strength. Amen.

AFTERWORD

A WORD TO THE NOBLE MOTHERS
AND WOMEN OF ISRAEL

EDITOR'S NOTE: *This essay by Fanny Neuda appears as an introduction to the first (1855) edition of* Hours of Devotion *and as an afterword, with changes, to all later German editions. Translated by Julia Watts Belser from the 1858 edition.*

Before these prayers are published, the one who compiled them cannot help but attach a word about a subject that is etched into the deepest reaches of human civilization and human destiny: *the raising of our daughters.*

The humbler the position a woman occupies in the public realm, the more meaningful is her position in the domestic sphere, and all the more influential and far-reaching is her effectiveness in her dual role as both wife and mother. For it is the wife who grants real value to her husband's life, and the wife who provides its true sanctification. Through her careful management, she brings the efforts of her husband to fruition as a rightful blessing. She adorns the house he builds and decorates it with her diligent, artful hand.

She turns it into a place filled with blessings, a place where friendship, kindness, gentleness, goodness, and charity reign. With gentle words she strives to banish all rancor and ill will from his brow and to uplift and sweeten all his hours of joy. Through her sensible speech she subdues her husband's easily inflamed temper and tries to influence his often unbending, implacable nature toward gentle and forgiving actions. She is a true companion in life's struggles, a consoling friend in hard times, and, above all, the caring angel of his being.

What a meaningful realm of action unfolds for a woman in her capacity as a mother! In truth, a woman's achievements as a mother, as the one who raises the children, carries immeasurable effects. Her sphere of influence extends out from the four pillars of her household to entire generations and families. In its first years of life, a child's heart is as soft as wax, ready to be molded and developed; and from whom else does a child receive her first impressions than from her tender mother, who is always there, who cares for her and tends to her every need. The mother's words are, for her child, those of an oracle; the mother's gaze, a heaven. Her singing, her speech, her admonitions, and her example penetrate every pore of the young soul and inspire within it a wellspring for good, for virtue, and for the religion that will bring the child comfort and well-being throughout her entire life. Through the streams of this wellspring, future generations will likewise be blessed. The father has no such power over his child's heart, for his occupation often keeps him far from home. His business interests and financial concerns too often hold his mind prisoner. But he also lacks gentleness, softness, and tranquility—the very qualities that are unique to the female spirit, under whose breath the tender little shoot of a child flourishes.

Yet only a woman of noble heart and cultivated mind can completely fulfill this holy dual occupation. Diligent guidance and upbringing are required for our daughters to be able to serve as priestesses—happily for themselves and bringing happiness to others—at the altars of their homes. Such an upbringing is a challenge that requires great skill, great cleverness, and, yes, even great wisdom, together with considerable tact and untiring perseverance. For just as one sows and plants a wide variety of seeds and seedlings in the furrows of the nurturing earth to draw forth manifold fruits and to draw out all of the land's potential for our good use, so, too, must one who raises a child tend the untilled ground whose care has been entrusted to her, sowing many seeds and bringing all the child's dormant strengths to fruition.

Just as we guide the young hand toward artistic needle-work and provide practice in the domestic arts and other practical occupations, so too must we strive to develop the free unfolding of the child's spirit. So while we devote our attention to industrious activity and adorn the child's mind with education, enriching it with knowledge of all kinds, we must not forget the actual foundation and cornerstone of all civilization, without which all knowledge and education are but a distant winter sun, a sun that shines and sheds light but offers no warmth, a sun whose brilliance is unable to nurture or awaken the field into bloom—this is *the ennobling of the heart, the development and strengthening of religious feeling.*

Today, unfortunately, this is completely neglected. We cultivate superficial glitter but neglect the heart with all of its blossoms and seeds. We leave it to time alone to see what will spring forth—sweet, nourishing fruits; weeds; or even poisonous plants. Religious education takes place only on the margins, treated merely as a minor matter. Yet nobility of feeling and deeply felt religiosity are a woman's highest ornaments. They shower her entire being with every endur-ing charm and grace that wins every heart; they alone grant all her qualities and talents their true worth. Only in con-cert with them do a woman's qualities become a real bless-ing for her home and for the world, for the past and for the future.

Therefore, you noble mothers of Israel, we must take

care that this highest adornment of our daughters not slip away. We must make it the first duty of those who educate our girls to ensure that, through the finest instruction, their hearts are ennobled by God's exalted teachings and wonders; that they are taught the full history and fate of our ancestors; that their souls are filled with pious, selfless connection to their people and a passionate love for humanity. We must accompany our daughters to the house of God, where sermons, songs, and worship can have an ennobling influence on the feminine nature, hallowing the emotions of young women and leading them to deeply honor God.

But for our daughters to participate in religious services in a successful manner, in a manner rich with blessings, so that the pious refrains and songs of our synagogues will play an ennobled and exalted melody on the heartstrings of the feminine soul, one great need remains above all—this is *the knowledge and understanding of our holy language of prayer*. For without this, we hear only words but not the Word. The sounds reach our ears but not our hearts, and we pray only with our lips, not with our souls. The hallowed songs of Zion, the heavenly psalms of David, the exalted, soulful prayers of the people of Israel are but a closed book to us.

For why should our daughters, who invest such time and energy learning to play the piano and to sing opera, who study languages that are fashionable and *en vogue* today, not also devote an hour each day to the learning of our holy tongue, the noble mother of all languages, the language that is the key to those treasures of the heart and mind that God set down in his Book, which we so appropriately call "the book of books"? Shouldn't they dedicate a small portion of their time to learning *the language* that remains the bond uniting all members of the Jewish people scattered throughout all the countries of the world? In all the regions of the earth—in Cincinnati and in Bombay, in Tunis and in Warsaw, in Vienna and in London—the language that God once spoke from Sinai still resounds from every Jewish temple.

These feelings of true feminine religiosity must be accompanied by an exalted feeling of national pride. Our daughters should learn to carry the name of Children of Israel with dignity and self-confidence. They should recognize the inner worth of their people and be aware that the afflictions that have marked the fate of many sad figures, and the antagonism and reproach that meanness or prejudice attempts to attach to us, will and must be washed pure in the stream of time. Our daughters should be aware that they would be devaluing themselves if they were ashamed of belonging to a people that is the equal of any in history—a people whose annals are rich with brilliant heroes, noble men, and courageous martyrs. It should be their consolation, their goal, and their joy to rise above all rebuke by the strength of their spirits and to prove themselves as the authentic daughters of a people that, despite a thousand-year struggle against all manner of deeply painful hostility, has nevertheless preserved the blessings of a joyous, domestic consciousness and a noble character.

We also want to pay special attention to our daughters' surroundings to guard that no deceitful words, no wounding treatment, disturb the pure harmony of their souls, that no impure breath tarnishes the clear mirror of their hearts.

How do we best protect the fresh, unfurling blossom of the innocent flower from the poison of corruption? We do so by strenuously protecting our daughters against company in which all topics are treated without consequence, in which God and holiness are treated frivolously or disrespectfully, in which the passion for right and truth are mocked, and in which the most exalted feelings are passed off as ridiculous—lest the holy spark within their young hearts suffocate, lest that brilliant beam of light that clarifies and illuminates their enthusiasms become darkened and obscured. So, too, must we absolutely keep them away from places where gossip creeps into all the cracks and crevices of other people's characters and into the fortunes of our dear neighbors, where it unsparingly exposes every speck and blemish, where the occupation of backbiting and spite rules. We must also protect them against [a social environment] in which the sound of flattering gallantry reigns and so accustoms the ear to the sweet sound of adulation that the vibrant sound of truth becomes painful by comparison; or even that kind of gallantry that calls up corrupting, arousing images in their souls and agitates their calm, steady heartbeats.

We must furthermore ensure that the plague of the century, the corrupting craving to read [popular] novels, does not win any power over them—this appetite to read everything, without choice or taste, including fabrications that stir up and overtax the imagination, confusing and weakening the notion of true, pure womanhood; creations in which the very offenses that deserve the strongest possible ban are permitted under the guise of tolerance and even cloaked in an aura of false prestige.

Of course, we want to introduce our daughters to other people, but only to those with whom their hearts may connect openly and joyfully and find a harmonious resonance. We must seek out an environment for them in which pure sincerity and a pious, innocent heart are valued and held inviolate, in which they will encounter the very embodiment of female worth and virtue in its most graceful form, inspiring them to imitation and emulation, and in which their mind's eye will be trained on all that is noble and beautiful.

And of course we should give them books, but books that have been carefully selected by the watchful, discerning eye of a sensible mother or teacher. We already have so many books that elevate and educate the heart and mind. Our day is rich enough in writings that flow from the pens of gifted authors who have as their goal the education and entertainment of young readers.

Above all, however, we must serve as noble examples of modesty and sufficiency, of domestic stewardship, of inner attachment to God and people and faith, and of loyal performance of all our duties, so that we may teach our daughters to find fulfillment and delight in the pursuit of a loftier goal than that of luxury and vain frills.

When our daughters' early upbringing receives such care, then we may be permitted to hope that good fortune will accompany them into their matrimonial houses, that joy and well-being will make permanent residence there, and that the spirit of peace and harmony, the spirit of generosity and inner, joyful religiosity, will rule within their homes.

Only the wealthy and those in higher social positions find it easy to acquire a full education for their daughters that builds and ennobles their minds and hearts. These families have the means to provide their daughters with diligent teachers who strive with wisdom and prudence for the betterment of their charges. Or they entrust their children to the guardianship of a girl's school where many teachers work together to give careful attention to the discharge of this important task, moving tirelessly and with determination toward their goal.

So are the rich provided for. But what about those with fewer resources? How can the poor—those who have an even more urgent need for quality teaching—begin to provide these things? Useful knowledge could help them become self-sufficient or lead them toward a better life, whereas without it they are likely to remain trapped in neediness and misery.

Therefore, if among all the humanistic inventions of our time it is the educational institutions for girls that have received the most recognition, and if their positive effects are unmistakable to all, the most praiseworthy of these institutions are those whose mission it is to take in poor students free of charge. Thus the benefits and blessings of their instruction are distributed equally on the rich and the poor, just as the sun bestows its life-giving rays in equal measure on the peaks and the valleys. The supporters of these institutions have created memorials that will immortalize them more surely than any monument of gold and marble.

Yet, regrettably, very few of our communities have such institutions. Therefore, I cannot help but express a wish that those philanthropists who care deeply about the welfare of the poor—who gladly bring a breath of fresh air and joy to the dim dwellings of the needy through pious charity, and who want to go beyond offering mere temporary assistance for their pressing hunger—help secure for them better prospects for the future: Let those warm and noble hearts come together to found just such institutions in their own communities. Let them energetically set to work on this noble, redeeming task and strive for it with great energy; and let this be the altar for their offerings to God, on which the Eternal One will certainly gaze down with blessings and with pleasure.

FANNY NEUDA

ACKNOWLEDGMENTS

My journey of reviving Fanny Neuda's prayer book has been blessed with the kindness and generosity of many individuals, each of whom has become an integral part of this project. First among these is my beloved teacher and friend, Ronnie Serr, whose wise guidance, encouragement, and practical help have lit the way for me from the beginning. This book would not exist without him. I am also deeply grateful to the Shir HaShirim community that Ronnie leads and especially to my dear friend Barbara Ratner, who offered perceptive feedback at every point.

Sincere thanks to my literary agent, Joe Spieler, for his faith in this project and his critical expertise, and to my editor, Deborah Garrison at Schocken Books, for guiding this book into being with grace and consummate skill. Thanks also to designer Gabriele Wilson for the exquisite jacket design and to everyone else at Schocken Books for their valuable contributions, including Avery Flück for production management; Altie Karper and Janice Goldklang for editorial direction; Victoria Pearson for editorial production; consultant Fred Wiemer for copyediting; Iris

Weinstein for the elegant interior design; and editorial assistant Caroline Zancan, who made every phase of this publication a pleasure.

I am deeply grateful to the principal translator of this text, Julia Watts Belser, whose depth of knowledge and affinity for the material were an ideal match for Fanny Neuda's work. Thanks also to Steven Lindberg for translating Fanny's preface, to Annelisa Stephan for copyediting the afterword, and to Yael Levine for offering research information.

I also wish to thank my colleagues at Getty Publications, particularly Rob Flynn, acting marketing manager, who kindly referred me to my agent; Mark Greenberg, editor in chief, for his wise counsel and support; Jim Drobka for technical help; and Stacy Miyagawa for being present to it all. Thanks also to Valerie Greathouse, librarian at the Getty Conservation Institute, for valuable bibliographic research.

My profound gratitude goes especially to Luděk Štipl, director of the Respect and Tolerance foundation in Loštice, Czech Republic, and to Hana Heiden Reichová, Lukáš Koval, and the others on their team for generously sharing their original research with me and for so warmly welcoming me to Loštice. I am also grateful to Dr. Stanton Canter, founder and principal sponsor of Respect and Tolerance, for his personal insights, and to artist Judith Joseph for putting me in touch with this remarkable organization. Thanks also to Prof. Josef Blaha at the University of Prague for introducing me to Prague's progressive Jewish community and to curator Olga Sixtová for kindly providing me access to the Jewish Museum in Prague.

I feel honored and blessed to have been able to study with so many wonderful teachers, especially Rabbi Mordecai Finley of Ohr HaTorah congregation, whose brilliant teaching continuously illuminates my mind and deepens my practice. I am also grateful for the teachings of Rabbis Emily Feigenson, Ivan Ickovits, T'mimah Ickovits, Jonathan Omer-

Man, Debra Orenstein, Zalman Schachter-Shalomi, David Seidenberg, Rami Shapiro, and Scott Shapiro; and for the ongoing spiritual sustenance of the Ohr HaTorah and Metivta communities.

I am especially grateful to Evelyn Baran and Alain Cohen for the generous use of their Ojai retreat, where much of this book was written; to Terry Braunstein, Melinda Grubbauer, and Sheri Saperstein for their creative advice and loving friendship; and to Curt Biren, David Braunstein, Ruth Broyde-Sharone, Barbara Crane, Donne Davis, Ann Dorr, Ruth Osborn, and Shannon Taylor for their unwavering support.

I have dedicated this book to my children, Adam, Jessica, and Rebecca Portner, who honor me with their ever-present love and confidence, which I never take for granted. I am also indebted to my daughter-in-law, Rachelle Indictor Portner, for her abiding faith in family and to my treasured friend Gary Kamisher for bringing the sweetness of Shabbat into all my days.

Above all, I thank God for delivering Fanny Neuda's book into my hands at exactly the right moment and for allowing me to become the vessel for its rebirth. May these prayers inspire your own.

D.B.

NOTES

SOURCE NOTES

The prayers and afterword included here are based on Fanny Neuda [née Schmiedl], *Stunden der Andacht: Ein Gebet-und Erbauungs-Buch für Israels Frauen und Jungfrauen zur öffentlichen und häuslichen Andacht, sowie für alle Verhältnisse des weiblichen Lebens* (Prague: Wolf Pascheles; G.L. Fritsche; Leipzig and Frankfurt: J. Kaufmann, 1855 [1st ed.], translated for this publication from the 1858 and 1914 editions by Julia Watts Belser; and on M[oritz] Mayer, trans., *Hours of Devotion: A Book of Prayers and Meditations for the Use of the Daughters of Israel, During Public Service and at Home, for All Conditions of Woman's Life* (New York: Hebrew Publishing Co., 1866, 5th ed.). Fanny Neuda's preface was translated by Steven Lindberg.

English translations of biblical epigraphs are based on the following sources:

Rabbi Samson Raphael Hirsch, trans. and commentary, *The Psalms*, new, corrected ed. Jerusalem and New York: Samson Raphael Hirsch Publications Society, Feldheim, 1997.

Rabbi Aryeh Kaplan, *The Living Torah: The Five Books of Moses and the Haftarot.* New York and Jerusalem: Maznaim, 1981.

Rabbi Nosson Scherman, ed., *Tanach—The Torah/Prophets/Writings: The Twenty-Four Books of the Bible Newly Translated and Annotated,* Artscroll ser., Stone ed. Brooklyn: Mesorah, 2003.

Tanakh: *The Holy Scriptures: The New JPS Translation According to the Traditional Hebrew Text*. Philadelphia and Jerusalem: Jewish Publication Society, 1985.

NOTES TO THE EDITOR'S PREFACE

1   This is the prayer title as it appears in the table of contents of the Mayer edition of *Hours of Devotion* (1866; see source notes). Above the prayer itself, the title is given as "A Mother's Prayer Whose Child Is in a Foreign Land" (Mayer, *Hours of Devotion*, p. 86). In this book, I have changed the title to "For a Mother Whose Child Is Abroad" (see p. 163).

2   Rabbi David A. Cooper, *God Is a Verb: Kabbalah and the Practice of Mystical Judaism* (New York: Riverhead Books, 1997); Roger Kamenetz, *The Jew in the Lotus: A Poet's Re-Discovery of Jewish Identity in Buddhist India* (New York: HarperCollins, 1995).

3   Rabbi Rami M. Shapiro, *Minyan: Ten Principles for Living a Life of Integrity* (New York: Bell Tower, 1997).

4   *The Jewish Encyclopedia*, www.jewishencyclopedia.com, 1901–1906, s.v. "Abraham Neuda."

5   See www.respectandtolerance.com. I am indebted to the Respect and Tolerance foundation, Loštice, Czech Republic, particularly Luděk Štipl, director, and Dr. Stanton Canter, founder and principal sponsor, for sharing their extensive research with me and helping me to further my own.

6   See www.judithjosephstudio.com.

7   Pauline Dubkin Yearwood, "Like Old Times: A Chicago Torah Visits Its Old Home in Europe," *Chicago Jewish News*, September 16, 2005, archived at www.chicagojewishnews.com. Thanks to Judith Joseph for sharing this article and to Stanton Canter and Respect and Tolerance for additional information.

8   As of this writing, Respect and Tolerance was engaging in further restoration of the building, thanks to a generous donation from the city of Loštice and other sponsors.

9   With gratitude to Respect and Tolerance for genealogical research of Fanny Neuda's family.

10   *Jewish Encyclopedia*, s.v. "Prossnitz"; and Ari Shapiro, trans., "Jewish Town of Prostějov," in Jaroslav Klenovský, *Židovské Město v Prostějově* [Jewish Town of Prostějov] (Brno-Prostějov, 1997), pp. 60–61. Thanks to PhDr. Marie Dokoupilová, curator at the Prostějov Museum, for providing me with a copy of this booklet, sharing photographs from the museum's archives, and

personally pointing out Jewish historical sites in the city of
Prostějov that indicate the once-substantial Jewish presence there.

11 *Jewish Encyclopedia*, s.v. "Adolf Schmiedl."

12 The name of the leader was changed in various editions over
time. The 1897 edition, published three years after the author's
death, names Franz Joseph II along with Queen Elizabeth: Neuda,
Stunden der Andacht (Prague: Jacob B. Brandeis, 1897), pp. 24–25.
The 1914 edition, published twenty years after her death and
bound with a standard German-Hebrew siddur, names "our father
the Emperor Wilhelm the Second," commander in chief of the
German armed forces in World War I, as well as Queen Victoria;
Neuda, *Stunden der Andacht* (Prague and Breslau: Jacob B. Bran-
deis, 1914), pp. 24–26. The 1936 Frankfurt version, edited by
Martha Wertheimer and published during the Third Reich,
offers a substantially abridged version of this prayer, titled
"Gebet für das Wohl der Heimat" [Prayer for the Welfare of the
Country], without naming a specific leader; Neuda, *Stunden der
Andacht: Ein Gebet- und Erbauungsbuch für Israels Frauen und Mädchen zur öffentlichen und häuslichen Andacht*, ed. Martha Wertheimer (Frankfurt: J. Kauffmann, 1936), p. 34. This shorter prayer
remained unchanged through the last printing of Wertheimer's
edited version in 1968; Neuda, *Stunden der Andacht* (Basel: Victor
Goldschmidt, 1968), p. 34.

13 A detailed, late-nineteenth-century history of these controversies
is given in H. Graetz, *History of the Jews*, vol. 5 (Philadelphia:
Jewish Publication Society, 1895), pp. 672–99.

14 Bernard Suler in Cecil Roth, ed., *Encyclopedia Judaica* (Jerusalem: Keter Publishing, 1971), s.v. "I. N. Mannheimer."

15 All quotations from Fanny Neuda's essay, translated for this volume by Julia Watts Belser, are from *Stunden der Andacht*, 2nd ed.
(Prague: Wolf Pascheles, 1858), pp. 143–52.

16 For a fascinating memoir exploring Jewish life in Moravia
and Bohemia, including excerpts from Fanny Neuda's essay
on teaching Hebrew to Jewish women as a means of repairing
their self-regard, see Helen Epstein, *Where She Came From: A
Daughter's Search for Her Mother's History* (New York: Plume,
1998), esp. pp. 57–59. For an in-depth discussion of female liter-
acy in nineteenth-century Eastern Europe, including the study of
Hebrew, see Iris Parush, *Reading Jewish Women: Marginality and
Modernization in Nineteenth-Century Eastern European Jewish Society*, trans. Saadya Sternberg, Brandeis Series on Jewish Women
(Waltham, Mass.: Brandeis University Press, 2004).

17 For more on Neuda's work in relation to the role of women as

instillers of religious values, see Susanne Blumesberger, "Fanny Neuda als Botin religiöser Literatur von Frau zu Frau; theologische Schriften für Frauen und Mädchen aus weiblicher Hand" [Fanny Neuda as the Messenger of Religious Literature from Woman to Woman: Theological Writings for Women and Girls by Women Authors], *Biblos: Osterreichische Zeitschrift für Buch- und Bibliothekswesen, Dokumentation, Bibliographie, und Bibliophilie* 52:1–2 (2003): pp. 7–21. I am grateful to Yael Levine for this reference.

18 As evidenced by a plaque to his memory in Loštice; Respect and Tolerance archives, Loštice, Czech Republic.

19 *Biographisches Handbuch der Rabbiner* (Munich: K. G. Saur, 2004), p. 682. Thanks to Luděk Štipl and the Respect and Tolerance foundation for this reference and translation.

20 *Biographisches Handbuch*, p. 682; and *Jewish Encyclopedia*, s.vv. "Abraham Neuda," "Isaac Noah Mannheimer," and "Nehemia Trebitsch (Menahem Nahum)."

21 Fanny Neuda, preface to original edition of *Hours of Devotion*. See herein, p. xlvi. Translated for this volume by Steven Lindberg.

22 See "Bibliographic record of *Hours of Devotion*," p. 285.

23 Census of 1857, Loschitz, Austria; State District Archive (SOkA), Šumperk, Czech Republic. A document notarized by Fanny's cousin Elias Karpeles verifies that the three sons, born in 1842, 1845, and 1846, are Abraham Neuda's. In addition, records show that the youngest son, Gotthold Neuda (b. May 20, 1846), traveled more than once from Brussels to the United States and was married in New York in 1888. It is hoped that ongoing genealogical research will yield more information about Fanny and Abraham's descendants. Thanks to Sheri Saperstein for her useful efforts in this direction.

24 Kartei der Fremden (Card index of foreigners), Vienna, 1880; thanks to Celia Male and Respect and Tolerance for this information.

25 *Naomi* (Prague, Leipzig, 1867); and *Jugend-Erzählungen aus dem israelitischen Familienleben* [Children's Stories from Jewish Family Life] (Prague, 1876; 2nd ed., 1890).

26 For more on *tkhine* literature, see Chava Weissler, *Voices of the Matriarchs: Listening to the Prayers of Early Modern Jewish Women* (Boston: Beacon, 1998), and Devra Kay, *Seyder Tkhines: The Forgotten Book of Common Prayer for Jewish Women* (Philadelphia: Jewish Publication Society, 2004).

27 The author of one such volume, published in 1828, was none other than Wolf Pascheles, who later became, along with his son-in-law Jacob B. Brandeis, the first publisher of *Hours of Devotion*

(1855); see www.jewishencyclopedia.com, s.v. "Wolf Pascheles." For more on the issue of male authorship of *tkhines*, see Weissler, *Voices of the Matriarchs*, esp. pp. 9–10, 36–37, and 81–82.

28 *Jewish Encyclopedia*, s.v. "Moritz Mayer."

29 For more on seventeenth-century prayer books for Jewish women, see Kay, *Seyder Tkhines*, and Weissler, *Voices of the Matriarchs*.

30 From two biographies of Fanny Neuda (both in German): Bettina Kratz-Ritter in Jutta Dick and Marina Sassenberg, eds., *Jüdische Frauen im 19. und 20. Jahrhundert: Lexikon zu Leben und Werk* [Jewish Women of the Nineteenth and Twentieth Centuries: Dictionary of Their Lives and Work] (Hamburg: Rowohlt, 1993), pp. 295–96; and Pnina Navè Levinson, comp., *Esther erhebt ihre Stimme: Jüdische Frauen beten* [Esther Raises Her Voice: Jewish Women Praying] (Gütersloh, Ger.: Gütersloher Veragshaus Gerd Mohn, 1993), pp. 180–81. For the development of Jewish women's prayer literature in German, see also Bettina Kratz-Ritter, *Für "fromme Zionstöchter" und "gebildete Frauenzimmer": Andachtsliteratur für deutsch–jüdische Frauen im 19. um frühen 20. Jahrhundert* [For "Pious Daughters of Zion" and "Educated Women": Devotional Literature for German Jewish Women in the 19th and early 20th Centuries] (Hildesheim, Ger.: Georg Olms Verlag, 1995).

31 Wolf Pascheles, publisher's preface to Fanny Neuda [née Schmiedl], *Stunden der Andacht* (Prague: Wolf Pascheles; Leipzig, C. L. Fritsche; Frankfurt: J. Kauffmann, 1855), p. viii.

32 Kratz-Ritter in Dick and Sassenberg, *Jüdische Frauen*, p. 296. Translated here by Julia Watts Belser.

33 Bettina Kratz-Ritter, " '. . . als das Ergebnis eines *weiblichen* Herzens': Beobachtungen zum Frauenbild im religiösen und belletristischen Werk Fanny Neudas (1819–1894)" [. . . "The Product of a *Female* Heart": Observations on the Image of Women in the Religious and Literary Work of Fanny Neuda], *Zeitschrift für Religions-und Geistesgeschichte* 47, 4 (1995): 357. I am grateful to Yael Levine for this reference.

34 Fanny Neuda, *Stunden der Andacht*, ed. Wertheimer.

35 Wertheimer in Neuda, *Stunden der Andacht*, ed. Wertheimer, p. 11.

36 WorldCat lists dozens of copies of various editions in libraries worldwide. I have purchased early copies from booksellers located in Argentina, the United Kingdom, the Netherlands, and cities across the United States.

37 Schorsch notes that the inside front cover of this copy contains the first names of family members and that the inside back cover records the death dates of his aunt's two brothers, who perished

in Theresienstadt in 1944; Ismar Schorsch and Jackie Feldman, "Memory and the Holocaust: Two Perspectives," in Harvey E. Goldberg, ed., *The Life of Judaism* (Berkeley: University of California, 2001), p. 154.

38   These include Marcia Cohn Spiegel and Deborah Lipton Kremsdorf, eds., *Women Speak to God: The Prayers and Poems of Jewish Women* (San Diego, Calif.: Women's Institute for Continuing Education, 1987), p. 26; Ellen M. Umansky and Diane Ashton, eds., *Four Centuries of Jewish Women's Spirituality: A Sourcebook* (Boston: Beacon, 1992), pp. 99–100; Levinson, *Esther erhebt ihre Stimme*, which contains excerpts of more than a dozen prayers in German; and Aliza Lavie, ed., *Tefilat nashim: Psifas nashi shel tefilot vesipurim* [Jewish Women's Prayers Through the Ages] (Jerusalem: Yedioth Ahronoth, Hemed, 2006), which contains a selection of Fanny's prayers translated from German to Hebrew.

39   Umansky in Umansky and Ashton, eds., *Four Centuries of Jewish Women's Spirituality*, p. 71 n. 14.

40   Although Mayer's translation was first published in 1866, the text on the title page reads: "Translated from the German '*Stunden der Andacht*' by M. Mayer, fifth edition." Judging from the bibliographic record, "fifth edition" probably means fifth in relation to all editions of *Hours of Devotion* to that date, not the fifth edition of Mayer's translation, and the higher edition number may have been assigned to give the book more credibility. See "Bibliographic Record of *Hours of Devotion*," herein, pp. 285–86.

41   Apparently such practices were not uncommon in the nineteenth century, before the advent of copyright laws. Among the prayers that differ from the German originals is "On the Approach of Childbirth," one of the most frequently anthologized in English. Another late-nineteenth-century translation of Fanny Neuda's prayer book—very rough at best—was published under the authorship of V. Vulture and titled *Hours of Devotion: Book of Prayer and Devotion for Israel's Women and Maids for Public and House Devotion as Well as for All Circumstances of Female Life* (Budapest: M. E. Loewy Son [1899?]). Although the title and table of contents closely follow German editions of *Hours of Devotion*, Fanny Neuda is not credited, nor is the German title given.

42   For more on *payyetanim* and the history of Jewish prayer, see Philip Arian and Ariel Eisenberg, *The Story of the Prayer Book* (Hartford, Conn.: Prayer Book Press, 1968), esp. pp. 86–96.

43   The English translations of these verses are based on a variety of

sources (see source notes). For the names of the divine, I have elected to use the Hebrew word **ADONAI** for יהוה, the ineffable name that signifies "existence" or "Source of Being," and to use "God" and "God's" for "He" and "His." Thanks to Ronnie Serr for reading the English biblical verses against the Hebrew and for providing the Hebrew text throughout.

44 Rabbi Samson Raphael Hirsch, introduction, *The Psalms*, new, corrected edition (Jerusalem and New York: Samson Raphael Hirsch Publications Society, Feldheim, 1997), pp. xi–xii.

45 In Kay's *Seyder Tkhines*, pp. 74–80, the author charts the framework of early prayer books for women in relation to the prayers in the siddur. Although *Hours of Devotion* only loosely follows the structure outlined there, and includes more prayers than in its Yiddish antecedents, the contents of Fanny's collection were clearly informed by the women's prayer books available during her time.

46 The early German printings of *Stunden der Andacht* are essentially the same after the 2nd (1858) edition, with the exception of the prayer "For the Leaders of Our Country" (see note 12). For reasons of typographical clarity, the source used for the translation of all the prayers in this book was the 23rd edition (Prague, Breslau: Jacob B. Brandeis, 1914).

BIBLIOGRAPHIC RECORD OF
HOURS OF DEVOTION

The following list was compiled from bibliographic databases and direct examination of various German editions of *Hours of Devotion* published between 1855 and 1968, the Yiddish edition of 1859, and English editions published in 1866 and 1899(?). Edition numbers shown here are as given in the bibliographic record or in copies of the books themselves.

Neuda (née Schmiedl), Fanny, *Stunden der Andacht: Ein Gebet-und Erbauungs-Buch für Israels Frauen und Jungfrauen zur öffentlichen und häuslichen Andacht, sowie für alle Verhältnisse des weiblichen Lebens* (in old German type, except as noted below) by date and publisher, as follows:

Prague: Wolf Pascheles; Leipzig: G. L. Fritsche; and Frankfurt: J. Kaufmann, 1855 (1st ed.)

Prague: Wolf Pascheles; Leipzig: G. L. Fritsche; Frankfurt: J. Kaufmann, Hamburg: R. B. Kaufmann; and Breslau: M. Monasch, 1858 (2nd ed.)

Prague: Wolf Pascheles, 1859 (in Yiddish), 1864, 1874

Prague: Jakob B. Brandeis, 1868 (6th ed.), 1886, 1888 (12th ed.), 1897 (16th ed.), 1899 (17th ed.), 1901 (18th ed.), 1903 (19th ed.), 1905 (20th ed.)

Prague, Breslau: Jakob B. Brandeis, 1908 (21st ed.), 1911 (22nd ed.),

1914 (23rd ed., bound with standard German-Hebrew prayer book), 1916 (24th ed.), 1917(?) (25th ed.), (ca. 1918) (26th ed.), 1918(?) (28th ed.)
New York: L. H. Frank, 1874 (10th ed.)
New York: H. Sakolski, 1882
Breslau: W. Koebner, 1890 (3rd ed.)
New York: Rosenbaum & Werbelowsky, 1890, 1893 (9th ed.)

————, M[oritz] Mayer, trans., *Hours of Devotion: A Book of Prayers and Meditations for the Use of the Daughters of Israel, During Public Service and at Home, for All Conditions of Woman's Life*, by date and publisher, as follows:
New York: Hebrew Publishing Co., 1866 (5th ed.), 1868
New York: J. L. Werbelowsky, 1866 (5th ed.)
New York: L. H. Frank, 1868 (1st ed.), 1870 (2nd ed.), 1872 (3rd ed.), 1875, 1878 (4th ed.), 1889 (5th ed.)
New York: H. Sakolski, 1882 (5th ed.)
Cincinnati: Bloch, 1886(?) (5th ed.)
New York: J. Rosenbaum, 1886 (5th ed.), 1889 (5th ed.)

————, R. Vulture, *Hours of Devotion: Being a Book of Prayer and Devotion for Israel's Women and Maids for Public and House Devotion as Well as for All Circumstances of Female Life* (Budapest: M. E. Loewy Son [1899?]).

————, *Stunden der Andacht: Ein Gebet- und Erbauungs-Buch für Israels Frauen und Mädchen zur öffentlichen und häuslichen Andacht*, revised and edited by Martha Wertheimer (Frankfurt: J. Kauffmann, 1936; Basel: V. Goldschmidt, 1950, 1959, 1968).

A NOTE ABOUT THE EDITOR

DINAH BERLAND is a poet and an editor with a background in art. Her poems have appeared in the *Antioch
Review, Ploughshares,* and the *Iowa Review,* and are anthologized in *Verse & Universe: Poems About Science and Mathe-
matics* and *Nice Jewish Girls: Growing Up in America,*
among other publications. She received her M.F.A. in
creative writing from Warren Wilson College and an
individual fellowship in poetry from the California Arts
Council. She lives in Los Angeles, where she works as a
book editor for the J. Paul Getty Museum. Dinah can be
contacted at www.dinahberland.com.

A NOTE ON THE TYPE

The text of this book has been set in Goudy Old Style, one of the more than one hundred typefaces designed by Frederic William Goudy (1865–1947). Although Goudy began his career as a bookkeeper, he was so inspired by the appearance of several newly published books from the Kelmscott Press that he devoted the remainder of his life to typography in an attempt to bring a better understanding of the movement led by William Morris to the printers of the United States.

Produced in 1914, Goudy Old Style reflects the absorption of a generation of designers with things "ancient." Its smooth, even color combined with its generous curves and ample cut marks it as one of Goudy's finest achievements.

COMPOSED BY
Creative Graphics, Allentown, Pennsylvania

PRINTED AND BOUND BY
R. R. Donnelley, Harrisonburg, Virginia

DESIGNED BY
Iris Weinstein